Courts
and Alleys

Courts
and Alleys

A history of Liverpool courtyard housing

Elizabeth J. Stewart

LIVERPOOL UNIVERSITY PRESS

First published 2019 by
Liverpool University Press
4 Cambridge Street
Liverpool
L69 7ZU

British Library Cataloguing-in-Publication
data
A British Library CIP record is available

ISBN 978-1-78694-211-1

Typeset by Carnegie Book Production
Printed and bound by TJ Books Limited,
Padstow, Cornwall, PL28 8RW

Cover photograph: A court off Beresford
Street in 1924
© Liverpool Record Office, Liverpool Libraries

To Jen McCarthy, deputy director of the Museum of Liverpool,
who loved telling people's stories

Contents

Preface and Acknowledgements

This book has been researched and written as part of the *Galkoff's and Secret Life of Pembroke Place* project (2016–19) run by Liverpool School of Tropical Medicine in partnership with the Museum of Liverpool. This project has been supported by the National Lottery Heritage Fund, thanks to National Lottery players. Research for this publication has also been supported by the Art Fund through a Jonathan Ruffer Curatorial Research Grant.

Thanks are due to the *Galkoff's and the Secret Life of Pembroke Place* project steering group and volunteer team who gathered a great deal of information about courts and the people who lived in them. Detailed information about court housing was gleaned from speaking to people with memories of this type of housing, through the *Our Humble Abodes* project run by Kerry Massheder-Rigby for the Museum of Liverpool. Special thanks to all the participants for sharing their stories.

Thanks to staff at Liverpool Libraries for assistance with document and image research. Particular thanks to Clare Cunliffe for her support, and for her assistance with photography and scanning. Thanks to Mark Adams, RSK, who supervised the Oakes Street excavation of court housing, and to Clare Cunliffe, Vanessa Oakden and Jeff Speakman for their work on the excavation and post-excavation analysis of the site.

Special thanks to Martyn Stewart, Poppy Learman, James Worth and Kerry Massheder-Rigby for all their help and support through the research and writing, and their patience with long discussions about 'slums'!

Children photographed in a courtyard by Liverpool city engineers
© Liverpool Record Office, Liverpool Libraries

Introduction

Court housing is a form of high-density housing found in British towns and cities from the eighteenth to the twentieth centuries. Courts, and associated cellar dwellings, were especially prevalent in Liverpool, and there is a range of historical evidence about them. Known as 'courts', 'alleys' and 'back houses', homes squeezed behind street-front properties provided additional accommodation in the town.

Court housing, and the people who lived in such accommodation, was the subject of press reports from the mid-nineteenth century. They featured in literature and in the speeches and books of reformers and social improvers (Walton and Wilcox 1991; Hocking 1880). First-hand descriptive accounts of Liverpool's court housing come from two main sources: public health officials, including Dr William Henry Duncan, the world's first Medical Officer of Health; and journalists, describing their town

in the nineteenth century. Some contemporary newspaper reports show a voyeuristic interest in the lives of the 'lower classes', part of the 'slumming' trend whereby middle-class people visited or read about visits to 'slums'. A sub-genre of literature also developed that represented the lives of the poor through novels, literary sketches, semi-biographical stories or observational texts (Koven 2004; Mayhew 1851; Booth 1898–99; Rowntree 1901). In Liverpool this would have been fuelled by the distinct division between the classes, especially as the housing of the poor declined into 'slums' and wealthier Liverpolitans moved away from the docks to areas that were under development, including Rodney Street, Abercromby Square and Everton Brow (Walton and Wilcox 1991; Simey 1951, 12). From 1801 the Liverpool courts are well recorded in census data which helps to develop a picture of the population density and living arrangements, and to understand more about the people living in courts.

Historic maps show the development and nineteenth-century extent of court housing across Liverpool, tracking the spread of the town, and later city, and the planned construction of courts as part of that. Photographs from the very late nineteenth and twentieth centuries provide an extensive source of information about life in the courts. There is just one surviving example of court housing in Liverpool, where the buildings can be investigated first hand: on Pembroke Place, the back rooms of two shops were originally three court homes. They are the truncated remains of two courts, which would originally each have contained eight houses. In 2018 the Museum of Liverpool undertook the first archaeological investigation of Liverpool court housing at Oakes Street, revealing information that will contribute to the wider archaeological study of workers' housing (Stewart et al. forthcoming; Nevell 2011; Symonds 2005; Walker and Beaudry 2011).

This book investigates the roots of this type of housing in the context of Liverpool's growth in the eighteenth and nineteenth centuries, and assesses why back-to-back and court housing became so prevalent. It explores life in Liverpool's courts, and reflects on the communities who lived in them, drawing on a range of sources. Finally, the impact of building control and the eventual clearance of court housing will be considered.

The growth of Liverpool

Liverpool developed around the 'pool', a natural tidal inlet convenient for the mooring of ships. It expanded as a commercial port through the seventeenth and eighteenth centuries, especially after the opening of its first dock in 1715, later known as the 'Old Dock'. The port was commercially highly successful, benefiting from its position as the primary maritime link between the industrial centres of north-west England and the Americas. Liverpool grew through mercantile trade, including the abhorrent trade in enslaved Africans and the products linked to it: sugar, tobacco and cotton.

Through the eighteenth and nineteenth centuries Liverpool 'boomed', the population growing rapidly due to natural increase – the birth of babies in the town – and inward migration. The growth fundamentally changed the place: 'Liverpool was transformed from a compact but important port to a modern sprawling city … This necessitated change in all aspects of the town: its physical fabric, economic structure, governance and population structure' (Pooley 2006, 171). Such growth demanded a huge increase in the housing stock, and speculative developers built new homes, filling in spaces and expanding the town. Letters published in 1845 on the *Unhealthy Condition of the Lower Class Dwellings* considered that 'there would be no better speculation for a man of capital, than to build tenements of the lowest class on a large scale', recommending that better conditions would, in fact, be more profitable in rental value (Girdlestone 1845, 1). Thousands of new homes were required in Liverpool, many for low-income families. Back-to-back housing provided an economical way of building homes which could be let for relatively low rents, but at a profit.

Courts and cellars provided

housing for the poorest people in eighteenth-, nineteenth- and early twentieth-century Liverpool. The population of the town increased massively in the late eighteenth and nineteenth centuries. There was a 300% increase from 165,175 in 1831 to 493,405 in 1871 driven by considerable inward migration from the surrounding counties, from Ireland, and from around the world, as well as by natural population growth (Honeybone 2007, 7).

As Liverpool developed, social structures became increasingly embedded in the physical arrangement of the place. The gulf between the urban elite and the urban poor was conspicuous, with minimal contact between the classes.

'In Liverpool, almost alone amongst the provincial cities of the kingdom, the intercourse between masters and men, between employers and employed, ceases on the payment of wages' (Trench, quoted in Simey 1951, 12). Some areas developed distinctive tendencies for certain types of housing: smaller workers' houses were common nearer the docks, while the historic central core of the town around Castle Street maintained a higher status. In some areas, however, homes of different size and quality were found in very close proximity. The 1835 Gage map, for example, shows the area around Great George Street, with both large grand houses and small courtyard houses immediately adjacent to one another.

Liverpool population increase, 1801–1931

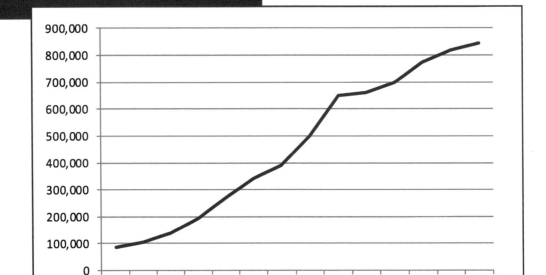

What is court housing?

'Courts' are compact streets of houses usually running at right angles to the main road. They were entered through a passageway from the main road, which opened on to a courtyard where houses faced one another across the open space. They were known as 'courts', 'courtyard houses', 'back houses' or 'alleys'. A typical plan had an ashpit and toilets at the end of the court away from the road, and from the mid-nineteenth century water piped to a standpipe in the centre. The courts were brick-built, some brickwork described as 'cheaply made with local clay', and roofed in slate where available, or tile (Pollard 1959, 18). The houses were usually built 'back to back' with those of the next court, so each home had a front door and windows to the courtyard, but no back door, as the back wall butted directly on to the next dwelling. There could be numerous parallel rows of courts along the length of a street. The courts and the houses themselves were often flagged, but some had bare earth floors, especially in cellars (Pollard 1959, 18; Burnett 1978, 75).

> In each of the longer courts there are usually 2 privies, with an ashpit between them, situated within three of four feet of the doors and windows of the houses at the upper end, and which are common property of all the houses in the court … a large surface of ground within and about these ill-ventilated courts and dwellings is constantly polluting the atmosphere with its noxious effluvia. (Duncan 1843, 13)

For developers and landlords, courts were relatively quick and easy to build, and produced high rents from a small area of land. They therefore became common in towns such as Liverpool as the population boomed in the nineteenth century and demand for housing increased.

Courts varied in size from two to around twenty houses, with the majority being between four and ten houses. In extreme cases early maps show warrens of courts and alleys behind street frontages containing over thirty houses. The buildings were two, three or four storeys high, and sometimes also had cellars. Cellar dwelling was more common in Liverpool than in many towns: in 1846 a total of 29,080 people were recorded as living in 7,577 cellars (Health of Town Committee 1846). Areas of each house would be sub-let so that a cellar or just one room might be home to an entire family. Prior to the construction of purpose-built court housing in eighteenth-century towns the lowest class of housing was formed from the subdivision and sub-letting of commercial, office and warehouse buildings to form tenement dwellings. Cellar dwelling within such buildings was deemed the worst-quality housing (Burnett 1978, 61).

Separate cellar housing led to severe overcrowding in some areas of the city. For example, when Hugh Shimmin, a journalist writing for the *Porcupine* newspaper in Liverpool, visited No. 2 Court, Hockenhall Alley off Dale Street in central Liverpool in 1863, he found three houses occupied by 50 people (Miller 1998, 3).

> There are about 160 houses in Henderson Street, and 25 inhabited courts on an average of four houses each. At a very moderate estimate you may allow seven persons for each house, and supposing each to be occupied – which fortunately is not the case at present – you would have in this street along a squalid population of at least 1,800 persons. (Shimmin 1883, 39)

Courts varied in quality and experience of life through time and across different areas of Liverpool. These differences were often based on the build quality of different houses: even houses built in close proximity at a similar period may have been very different in their construction. Better-built houses had the potential to provide dryer, warmer and more comfortable homes. However, even better-built houses could provide terrible living conditions if they were severely overcrowded or badly maintained.

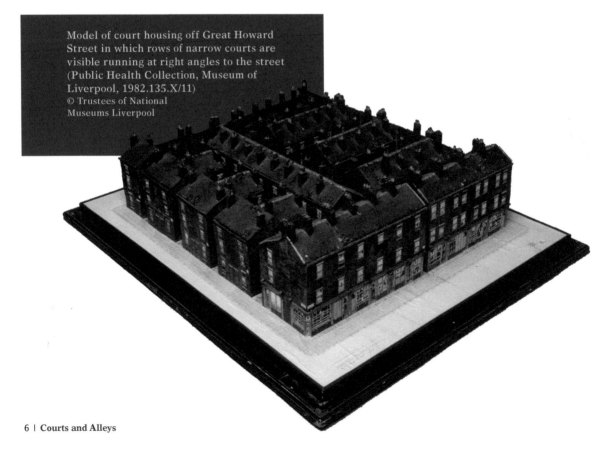

Model of court housing off Great Howard Street in which rows of narrow courts are visible running at right angles to the street (Public Health Collection, Museum of Liverpool, 1982.135.X/11)
© Trustees of National Museums Liverpool

The development of court housing

There were two types of court housing: 'closed courts', also known as 'arched courts', and 'open courts'. Closed courts were entered through a passageway from the street which opened on to a courtyard that was open to the sky, from which the houses were entered; they were a denser, darker and poorer type of housing than open courts. Though open courts were built in the late eighteenth and early nineteenth centuries, the closed type was more common as they were more profitable. An assessment in 1863 found that in north Liverpool, of 673 courts, 447 were closed at the upper end and 226 were open.

The standard layout of court houses in Liverpool was described in detail by James Newlands, the Borough Engineer, following his visits to courts as a public health inspector in 1858:

> The houses are generally built back to back, one end of the court as a rule is closed either by houses, or, which is worse, by the privies and ashpits, or a worse state of things still, the privies and ashpits are placed at the entrance of the court, and the only air supplied to the inhabitants must pass over their foul contents. (Newlands 1863, 25)

The earliest examples of back-to-backs arranged to create court housing were in open spaces behind larger houses, with an entrance only being provided through the front house – there were no pre-planned passageways through these buildings – meaning that the courts were 'closed' to the street frontage. The houses constructed in these yards varied in size and layout depending on the available space. The shapes of plots on which such housing was built was not standard. Early courts were often connected to rear access alleys, utilising any accessible space, and creating networks of back streets which grew more complicated as building continued in these areas (Burnett 1978, 73).

> There are courts which, by a perverted ingenuity, have been formed in this manner:– An ordinary street house has had its lobby converted into a common passage leading to a back yard. The passage is, of course, roofed over, and is, in fact, a tunnel from which the back room of the original house, now converted into a separate dwelling has its entrance. The back yard has been filled with other houses in such a manner as to only have the continuation of the tunnel for access, and from this little area of 3 feet wide the houses receive their supply of light and air. The passage is generally terminated

by a privy and ashpit common to all the wretched dwellings, with its liquid filth oozing through their walls, and its pestiferous gases flowing into the windows of the last two houses. The structural evils of these miserable abodes are aggravated by the filthy habits of its occupants. 'What is everybody's business is nobody's business' and so the duty of keeping the court and its conveniences clean is neglected. Even when the middens have been filled so as to overflow the court, no one cared to take the trouble to apprize the officers of the Nuisance Department of the fact in order to their being emptied. To those not conversant with the subject, it may appear that the evils of the courts and alleys life are exaggerated ... but ... in the Borough there are 3,723 courts, containing 18,610 dwellings; that the average number of houses in a court is 5.86, and the average number of inhabitants to a house is a fraction more than six; and it will be found that upwards of a fifth of the population of Liverpool is condemned to live in these morally and physically unwholesome dwellings. (Newlands 1863, 25)

As Liverpool expanded street planning started to include court housing as an integral element of the layout. Direct access from the street via a passageway was provided, and lines of back-to-backs were constructed as units. The plans of courts were increasingly formalized by the late eighteenth century (Taylor 1970, 77), and became yet more standardized in the first half of the nineteenth century. Back-to-back housing in regular court blocks spread across large areas of Liverpool. When built in the town, each back-to-back court house was of very small plan. Regularly spaced, equally sized courts of 10–15 feet wide with about eight houses around them became a common form for row after row in some areas of the town.

Hugh Shimmin (1819–79)

Hugh Shimmin was a journalist and editor of Liverpool's *Porcupine* newspaper from 1860. He was born in the Isle of Man, and moved to Liverpool in his childhood. Shimmin's father was an alcoholic who died young, leaving him to support his mother (Walton and Wilcox 2004). This shaped Shimmin's views on drinking, which are often evident in his judgmental writing about people living in court houses. Shimmin completed an apprenticeship as a bookbinder, and in the 1840s bought a bookbinding business. He started writing in the 1850s, gaining a reputation for his moralistic reports about local people and lifestyles. 'Shimmin said little about working conditions and practices, or about ethnic and sectarian divisions. He resisted the contemporary temptation to blame the Irish for social problems. He ascribed social ills to individual failings, although not solely to working-class ones' (Walton and Wilcox 2004). Shimmin's published descriptions of court housing, and the people he met there and events he witnessed, are among the most detailed surviving accounts of the social context of the places.

'The dismal courts, and wretched crumbling streets, some of which by the way – Sawney Pope Street, for example – contained, many years ago rather fashionable residences, are now inhabited by a hand-to-mouth living population of the most extraordinary description'

2

Where was court housing built?

Courts were mainly built in northern England and the midlands. There were also courts in London, where they were sometimes known as 'rookeries'. Some of the earliest examples of back-to-back housing are in rural settings where it was used to limit building costs. The shift of back-to-back housing from a rural setting to an urban environment must have seemed an obvious development, driven by the demand for housing in the rapidly growing towns of northern England. Rural and earlier urban back-to-back housing had represented relatively high-quality vernacular building (Crouch 2000, 52–8). The proliferation of many back-to-backs in northern English towns from the nineteenth century was seen throughout the north of England (Timmins 2013). Through the nineteenth century the development of high-density housing, which soon became overcrowded, rapidly brought courts into the classification of 'slum' housing.

As the population of towns and cities in northern England swelled during the nineteenth century, court housing was a common solution to the need for accommodation for the growing population. By the mid-nineteenth century Liverpool had swathes of court housing, laid out across large areas of the city, and possibly more cellar dwellings than any other British city of the period, but this type of housing was by no means unique to Liverpool. Houses built around courtyards were to be found in many other British cities, especially where the population had grown rapidly and space was infilled to provide new housing. Related types of housing could also be found in some North American cities, in some rapidly developing European cities, and in the Hutongs of Beijing in the nineteenth century.

Contemporary commentators highlight the fact that courts and cellar dwelling were especially common in northern and midland English urban areas, particularly in Liverpool, Birmingham and Manchester. Densely packed houses behind street-front properties were to be found across Britain (Upton 2005, 12–13).

Much of the high-density housing built to accommodate the rapidly growing urban population of Britain in the eighteenth and nineteenth centuries generated similar problems relating to its impact on public health. There have been archaeological excavations of workers' housing in a number of cities, including Glasgow (Nevell 2016), York (Connolly 2011) and Manchester (Nevell 2011). These have revealed a range of types of housing including back-to-backs, cellars and courts. Nevell found housing in Manchester in the eighteenth century comparable in size and levels of access and social control to contemporary rural housing (Nevell 2011, 598). However, increased pressure on space changed the conditions of much workers' housing in the nineteenth century. The archaeology of households reveals intensive habitation by thriving communities

'more concerned with the everyday problems of domestic and work life [than maintaining houses]' (Nevell 2011, 600).

Northern England

As the 'shock city' of the Industrial Revolution, Manchester and its living conditions attracted considerable contemporary comment and description (Nevell 2014). Friedrich Engels and J. P. Kay described life there, including the housing, and campaigned for better conditions for workers (Engels 1845; Kay 1832). These writings, though highly politicized, were a reflection of the physical surroundings that they documented. They especially described cellar dwellings, marking them as a type of housing almost exclusive to the Irish immigrants in Manchester, and characterizing them as overcrowded, squalid and breeding grounds for disease. Kay lists a catalogue of conditions which led to the prevalence of disease and high mortality: 'uncleanliness of the person, the street, and the abode; an atmosphere contaminated whether from want of ventilation, or from impure effluvia; extreme labour, and consequent physical exhaustion; intemperance; fear; anxiety; diarrhoea, and other diseases' (Kay 1832, 13). Engels describes the trap people found themselves in, having few options for housing: 'The working-man is constrained to occupy such ruinous dwellings because he cannot pay for others, and because there are no others in the vicinity of his mill' (Engels 1845, 58).

Back-to-back and court housing was common in Leeds, becoming a popular form of housing. Following popular resistance to building control, the construction of back-to-backs was only outlawed in 1909 (Harrison 2017). Excavations at Hungate in York explored the thousand-year history of the site, and in the modern era found nineteenth- and twentieth-century housing, and external toilets. In parallel to the Oakes Street site in Liverpool, the housing in the area had been demolished as part of 'slum clearance' and replaced with light industrial buildings (Connolly 2011).

In the smaller towns of northern England there was also rapid population increase in the nineteenth century, creating demand for homes (Forster 1972). In Birkenhead there was court housing, which the town corporation worked to remove in the late nineteenth century (Vacher 1882, 30). In Lancaster, numerous yards, lanes and alleys contained small houses. Historic maps and photographs taken in the late 1920s show court housing both in the centre of the town and in Skerton to the north.

The midlands

Court housing developed in midland towns including Birmingham, Coventry and the village of Atherstone (Alcock 2005, 49–60). In 1844 the *State of Large Towns Report* recorded that in Birmingham, 'a very large proportion (not less than 49,016…) reside in courts, or villages as they are termed by the inhabitants' (Commissioners for Inquiring into the State of Large Towns and Populous Districts 1844, 144). However, cellar dwelling was not found in Birmingham when research was undertaken in the 1840s: 'the absence of cellar dwellings in Birmingham, as well as the dry soil on which the town is situated, lessen the intensity of the evils to which the poor are exposed' (Commissioners for Inquiring into the State of Large Towns and Populous Districts 1844, 106). The vast majority of courts in the midlands have been demolished, but their form and character have been established from maps, photographs and census data (Alcock 2005, 49–60). The National Trust's 'Birmingham Back to Backs' is now an important heritage site of this type of housing, with individual houses reconstructed to show different phases of the buildings' history. This preserved example has the courtyard running parallel with the street, and the houses backing on to street-front shops, so the layout is different from that of a standard Liverpool court, but it still utilizes space behind street-front buildings to create housing around a courtyard.

Southern England

Examples of back-to-back and court housing have also been identified further south, including in Bristol, Ipswich and Reading, but broadly 'their existence south of Birmingham was exceptional' (Wohl 1977, 13, 135). London's nineteenth-century population growth was very rapid, from around 850,000 at the start of the century to over six million by the end. As elsewhere, new high-density housing was established. Here, courts and alleys were sometimes known as 'rookeries', possibly linked to their association with crime and 'rooks' or 'crooks'. Photographs and literary descriptions suggest significant parallels in living conditions to the northern courts, but in London, some buildings seem to have been more *ad hoc*,

shanty-like, and not always part of the formal plan for the development of the city (Guillery 2004).

The social campaigner Charles Booth visited London's courts, for example visiting Red Lion Street, and noting 'Taylor's rent on the East side … sack makers working at home – very poor not clean – tap in court – entered under arch way' (Booth 1898/99). In the 1880s Booth created a poverty map of London. At this time court and back-to-back housing was found in large areas of Liverpool and other northern cities, but it was not found so frequently in London, even in the poorest areas, which were classified by Booth in derogatory terms as 'vicious and semi-criminal'.

The courts that existed in London attracted the attention of writers. Henry Mayhew records the areas where courts were found:

> in Rosemary Lane … little courts and alleys spring from each side. Some of these courts have other courts branching off them, so that the locality is a perfect labyrinth … As you walk down 'the lane' and peep through the narrow openings between the houses … the court appears bright with the daylight; and down it are seen rough-headed urchins running with their feet bare, and bonnetless girls, huddled in shawls. (Mayhew 1851, vol. I, 109)

In some cases writers describe the geographical origins of communities: 'St. George's-in-the-Borough, with its back courts, where the refuse of Ireland vegetate' (Beames 1852, 133). Beames here reflects the prejudice and discrimination that would characterize references to the Irish community throughout the following century. Some writing presents housing conditions in disgusting detail: 'We enter a narrow court, picking our way with caution over the nameless filth and garbage and the decaying vegetable matter that, flung originally in heaps outside the doors, has been trodden about by the feet of the inhabitants' (Simms 1889, 119).

Scotland

Courts were less common in Scotland than they were in England, but some existed until the late nineteenth century. Following the City Improvement Scheme of 1866, Glasgow adopted a more formal plan for the development of the city and housing within it, and tenements started to become a common housing type, often replacing 'slum' dwellings, including courts. In advance of this work the City Improvement Trust commissioned the photographer Thomas Annan to capture images of some of the 'slum' housing in the city, including court housing which had grown up in the eighteenth and nineteenth centuries, sometimes incorporating earlier buildings.

'The inhabitants of
Liverpool live more
closely crowded together
than in most towns …
so many inhabitants
in so small a compass'

3

Back-to-backs and courts

Courts were a form of back-to-back housing. Back-to-back houses incorporate homes under a shared roof with a dividing spine wall, the houses accessed from opposite sides of the building. They therefore have no back door, the rear wall of the house being shared with the house behind. Back-to-back layouts were utilized in both urban and rural areas of northern England by the early eighteenth century. It was a type of housing that was easy to build and efficient as a means of accommodating numerous separate families or groups of people, and providing security. It was sometimes built at split levels to accommodate steep ground in a back-to-earth form, with entrances at two different levels on the two sides of the building (Burnett 1978, 72–3; Crouch 2000, 52–8). Back-to-backs provide compact accommodation, and are therefore economical in the use of building materials, with multiple shared walls. The vast majority of courts had houses which were back-to-back with houses in the next court: 'the court system was almost inseparable from back to back' (Burnett 1978, 73).

Historians of vernacular architecture have seen the development of back-to-back housing as a progression from some designs of rural homes: 'the design stems from that of earlier cottages which had only one entrance' (Barley 1963, 61). In Merseyside back-to-backs were built in some areas that were still rural in character, such as Wallasey, where some back-to-back cottages were constructed in the mid-nineteenth century. Back-to-back houses were more commonly built in larger groups or terraces. 'Court and back to back housing was inherited from pre-industrial housing designs and suited the necessity for high density low cost housing in the growing cities of late eighteenth and nineteenth century Britain' (Burnett 1978, 73). The introduction of back-to-back housing into spaces behind street-front houses in cities has been viewed as a logical use of open space when there was pressure for cheap housing close to areas of employment (Simey 1951, 11). It was a response by speculative builders to the growing population of towns such as Liverpool, who were in search of cheap housing.

The development of court housing was closely linked with the introduction of back-to-back housing to urban contexts. The earliest mention of back-to-back housing is in Bermondsey in south London in 1706. In the eighteenth century court houses were commonly known as 'back houses', those at the back of street-front properties. The earliest mention of court-style housing is in 1708 in Liverpool, when a rate book records eight 'back houses', and eight cellars were recorded as being in use as dwellings from 1705 (Taylor 1970, 76). The eighteenth century saw the proliferation of both court and cellar housing. By 1798 there were 1,608 back houses in Liverpool and 1,728 cellars were inhabited by 6,780 people, 12.6% of the population (Taylor 1970, 73–5).

Identifying exactly when courts developed as a widespread and distinctive housing type in Liverpool is difficult. Without censuses for the eighteenth century we are reliant on street directories to map the detail of the use of space within the city. In 1789–90 Makin Simmons conducted a survey of Liverpool's population and housing in his role as Overseer of the Poor (Laxton 1981, 75–95). Although complications in his recording have been identified, this is a valuable source, especially when compared to the Gore business entries and Richard Horwood's 1803 plan of Liverpool (Laxton 1981, 78–98). These records, together, helps us understand the very rapid growth in population in Liverpool in the 1790s and the increased prevalence of high-density housing to meet the demands of a growing number of people searching for accommodation (Laxton 1981, 96–7).

Many early maps of Liverpool do not provide sufficient detail to identify housing types specifically, so it is difficult to assess the prevalence of different housing types before the census data recorded street names. However, cellar dwellings were common enough by the 1780s that there were campaigns against the use of cellars as homes (Rosen 1993, 129). This probably reflected the growth in this type of accommodation – an increase of 30% in that decade alone (Taylor 1970, 79). This evidence and that of the first census in 1801 suggest that the framework of street-front houses with courts behind and the sub-letting of cellars were well established by the beginning of the

nineteenth century, growing as the population did through that century (Pooley 2006, 176).

The Simmons population record and the first census of 1801 divide Liverpool into districts, as is common practice in later records, and then divides areas into housing types: front houses, back houses (a term which often referred to courts) and cellars. This was not a methodology required for the census records, but rather reflected the primary housing types in Liverpool and the interests and concerns of the period in the types of buildings

people were calling 'home' (Laxton 1981, 79). The construction of courts in rapidly growing towns such as Liverpool was rapid, and by the time of the 1801 census, over 9,000 people in Liverpool lived in court housing, with a further 8,000 living in cellars (Laxton 1981, 80; Pooley 2006, 176). As the number of court and cellar dwellings increased, so did the discrepancy between the better housing and the poorer in terms of services, ventilation, light and population density. In 1801 the average number of people in a house in Liverpool was 6.6 in the borough as a whole, but there was far greater density of people in the central areas, with, for example a density of 7.3 people per house in Pitt Street, including those living in cellars (Pooley 2006, 176).

By the mid-nineteenth century the tightly packed nature of court housing in northern England was a point of interest for social commentators and visitors. 'All Salford is built in courts or narrow lanes, so narrow that they remind me of the narrowest I have ever seen, in the little lanes of Genoa' (Engels 1845, 62).

Why back-to-backs, courts and alleys?

In the compact eighteenth- and early nineteenth-century port town of Liverpool, where the population was growing rapidly, speculative building of housing for working-class people was a lucrative proposition. The move towards the widespread construction of court housing was the result of judgements by prospective developers on the market for housing, balanced against the cost of land and building (Taylor 1976, 121–5; Chalklin 1974).

Land costs were high, especially near the docks, necessitating high-density housing to return a profit on investment in buying land and building (Taylor 1976, 124). 'The houses are packed closely together

with an ingenious economy of space which does credit to the builders, though Liverpool has little reason to be thankful for it' (Parkes and Sanderson 1871, 63). The economic drive for this type of housing shaped the urban character of Liverpool and the housing experience for many thousands of people for over two centuries. 'The inhabitants of Liverpool live more closely crowded together than in most towns … It is probable that there is no place in Great Britain except London and Edinburgh which contains so many inhabitants in so small a compass' (Enfield 1773, 25). Where relatively high rents were charged for homes in the most accessible areas, there was also increased likelihood of sub-letting and lodgers, again increasing population density.

Speculative builders were able to fill their land with large numbers of houses to increase the profit from rents. Taylor's investigation of the courts around Crosbie Street has identified the developers. The people who owned the courts and received the rents were some of the powerful and wealthy politicians and merchants of Victorian Liverpool, members of the mercantile class. Several of these landowners were also involved in the trade in enslaved Africans, such as William Crosbie and Sir Foster Cunliffe (Taylor 1970, 79–81).

Many areas of Liverpool court housing were built in swathes by speculative builders, creating standardized rows of courts behind streets across large areas, especially in north Liverpool. However, areas such as Kitchen Street, near the central docks, developed more informally, with alterations and additions creating severe problems in terms of provision of services, ventilation and light. Courts sometimes developed more organically into non-standard forms, with sections being built in stages and linked together. This gradually produced warrens of alleys in the areas behind the main roads.

Missionary Buildings off Oakes Street, excavated in 2018, was built in two phases, mapping evidence showing that the west side was completed by 1835, while the east side was probably added in the early 1840s. This court was built on an unusual L-shaped plan, and linked

Entrance to a court off Burlington Street
© Liverpool Record Office, Liverpool Libraries

via an alley to the adjacent Anson Terrace. The construction of these buildings was revealed during the excavation as being of poor quality (Stewart et al. forthcoming).

While the quality of court buildings varied, some was certainly rapidly and poorly built. Writing in 1883, Hugh Shimmin describes courts off Bevington Bush, called Gildart's Gardens: these, he said, were 'in a condition more dangerous than usual. Many of the walls can hardly stand much longer, and some day will tumble with a crash' (Shimmin 1883, 31). Liverpool started to gain a reputation for poor-quality building, and it has been shown that the term 'jerry built' was first used around the 1830s in Liverpool (Sharples 2017, 3–4). It certainly became closely associated with Liverpool: 'jerry building, for which Liverpool is rather celebrated' (Stowell Brown 1858). The root of the term is unknown, but is potentially linked to the naval term 'jury' for a temporary or insubstantial repair to a ship's rigging – a term in use from at least 1788 (*OED*).

A peak in the construction of new court housing was reached in 1844–46. This was partly in response to the influx of new people to the town, including the growing Irish population, many arriving in Liverpool as a result of the Great Hunger. Another driver for rapid construction in this period was the anticipation of the introduction of building regulations, which might potentially decrease profit margins for speculative builders. From the 1860s land values began to make tenement-style buildings more profitable (Burnett 1978, 16).

Courts and back houses in New York

While court housing is a phenomenon of northern English cities, there are some international parallels. Houses built around courtyards, usually individual properties, are common across the world, creating secluded, shaded and secure outdoor spaces within a home. The use of spaces behind buildings on formal street layouts is also employed across the world in urban areas where pressure on space is paramount.

Grove Court, Greenwich Village, Manhattan, built 1848

When a report was commissioned on the *State of the Health of Towns in England* in 1844, comparison was drawn with New York, where there had been comparable population growth to Liverpool, and where similar solutions in building accommodation behind street-front properties were starting to be employed. Greenwich Village developed in the seventeenth century, with the street layout evolving to include courts from the nineteenth century. The area still contains examples of 'courts', low-rise housing around gated courtyards or on cul-de-sacs, which were tucked behind existing buildings as space became scarce.

Courts were also built in other American cities including Philadelphia and Baltimore (Herman 2005, 207–12). New York's population continued to soar into the later nineteenth century, and larger tenement houses were constructed to accommodate the growing number of people in the city. Even with these larger, taller buildings, the use of the space behind street-front properties continued, with 'back houses', often accessed through street-front apartment blocks, being built in the spaces behind.

'Liverpool, with all its commerce, wealth, and grandeur yet treats its workers with the same barbarity. A full fifth of the population, more than 45,000 human beings, live in narrow, dark, damp, badly-ventilated cellar dwellings'

4

Cellar dwelling

As Liverpool's population grew, people became more desperate to use every available space within buildings, and landlords became increasingly willing to let spaces, including cellars. Cellars were included in many eighteenth- and nineteenth-century houses for storage. Some large merchants' houses would have had the mixed functions of home and warehouse, keeping goods close as an added security measure. These storage spaces began to be used by the late eighteenth century as domestic accommodation:

> large and extensive cellaring built to afford warehouse room for merchandise, and it appears to have been general for the houses of mediocrity have also cellars which give residence to families and are generally let out by the owners of houses to many people following trades. This is certainly injurious to the health of inhabitants. (Wallace 1797, 81)

By the late eighteenth century cellars were providing a significant amount of Liverpool's accommodation. Simmons's enumeration (a local precursor to the census) records in 1789–90 that 19.4% of the town's cellars were inhabited, and provided homes for 12.6% of the population (Taylor 1970, 43). Similarly in 1798, Currie's report into the causes of typhus estimated that about 7,000 people, around 10% of the population, lived in cellars (Currie 1798, 222). This is again supported by the 1801 census.

While cellar dwelling in Liverpool probably initially developed because of the availability of storage cellars originally intended for goods (Taylor 1970), cellars were probably also built with the intention (even if not explicit) of their being let. The housing situation in Liverpool, especially the common cellar dwellings, shocked contemporary visitors, including Friedrich Engels, who wrote, 'Liverpool, with all its commerce, wealth, and grandeur yet treats its workers with the same barbarity. A full fifth of the population, more than 45,000 human beings, live in narrow, dark, damp, badly-ventilated cellar dwellings ... inhabited exclusively by proletarians' (Engels 1845, 36).

Cellars were sometimes within courts, and are inseparable from court housing in their development as part of the high-density housing of the industrial towns of northern England.

> The houses, both in streets and courts, are very generally sub-let, such room being sometimes occupied by one or more families; so that it is not uncommon to see an apartment 10 or 12 feet square, and perhaps, still more frequently, a cellar of the same dimensions inhabited by 12 or 14 human beings. (Duncan 1843, 19)

Court housing with cellars accommodated between 630 and 1,000 people per square acre, a very high population density, which made this type of housing very profitable to landowners and developers. A shift to other housing types was delayed until legislation enforced it (Sutcliffe 1974, 14).

Currie found that this housing and the density of people living in it contributed to high levels of typhus: 'Among the inhabitants of the cellars, and these back houses, the typhus is constantly present, and the number of persons under this disease that apply for medical assistance to the charitable institutions, the public will be astonished to hear, exceeds 3,000 annually' (Currie 1798, 222). The habitation of cellars grew as the town did, and by the 1840s Duncan estimated the population living in cellars as being over 20,000 (Duncan 1843, 11). Living conditions in cellars, sometimes without adequate furniture, could be dire:

> In the year 1836–7 I attended a family of 13, twelve of whom had typhus fever, without a bed in the cellar, without straw or timber shavings – frequent substitutes. They lay on the floor, and so crowded that I could scarcely pass between them ... yet amidst the greatest destitution and want of domestic comfort I have never heard during the course of twelve years' practice, a complaint of inconvenient accommodation. (Chadwick 1842, 19)

Cellars became an area of especial concern for public health officials. In his notebook records, Edward Hope, Assistant Medical Officer of Health, recorded cases of illness that he found during his visit, noting whether the patients were living in a cellar (Hope 1883–88). Hope's descriptions record cellars as among the most unhealthy of living conditions.

As with court housing, there

were better and worse examples of cellar dwellings. Those in Liverpool tended to be small, and sometimes unflagged, making them damp and dirty. The worst examples had no windows, and light entered only through the doorway and a grate or skylight to the street. Cellars were cramped, and were often used by elderly, poor widows and spinsters.

> There is frequently no window, so that light and air can gain access to the cellars only by the door, the top of which is often not higher than the level of the street . . . There is sometimes a back cellar, used as a sleeping apartment, having no direct communication with the external atmosphere, and deriving its scanty supply of light and air solely from the first apartment. (Duncan 1843, 11)

Cellar dwelling was not unique to Liverpool; it was found, for example, in Birmingham. However, it was not as common in other cities as in Liverpool (Simey 1951, 11; Taylor 1970, 73). In a comparative study in 1845, John H. Thom found that cellar dwelling was common in Liverpool, 'whilst in Birmingham no such thing could be discovered as a human being living in a cellar' (Thom 1845). Cellar dwelling is also recorded in Bradford and Salford. A description from Sheffield looking back to the nineteenth century explained that 'the cellar was not normally inhabited. The daily activities of the family were concentrated in the living-room, which served as kitchen, scullery, dining-room, living-room, as wash-room and bathroom, and on wet days, the clothes were hung up in it to dry' (Pollard 1959, 18).

Cellars were thought of as extra living space. In rare circumstances, families lived in cellar spaces out of choice, leaving the ground floor room for best, 'scarcely ever used, except perhaps on Sunday' (Hole 1866, 43–4). There are recorded cases of cellars being used as shared accommodation for newly arrived immigrants (Burnett 1978, 60). Living in cellars was generally disparaged, and Hugh Shimmin found, on visits to courts in the 1880s, that 'The inhabitants of houses everywhere will assert positively and emphatically that only one family resides in the house, and that the cellar, "is only used for washing"' (Shimmin 1883, 15).

In Liverpool there seem to have been areas with greater use of cellars for habitation, where the population density was especially high. 'The area around Tithebarn Street and Great Crosshall Street provided the nucleus from which a good deal of overcrowding occurred. Court and cellar dwellings which had already been built in the area' (Miller 1988, 12). Many of the inhabited cellars were in the area of the former infilled pool, around

Whitechapel, so flooding was a considerable risk.

It seems that people seldom stayed in cellars for a prolonged period, and tracing families and individuals from one census to another sees them moving within Liverpool. James and Jane Rooney, for example, lived in Shadwell Street in the 1871 census, had moved to a cellar in 24 Luton Street by the 1881 census, and were in a different cellar in Lincoln Street by the 1891 census. They had three children, one of whom died before she reached her teens.

Cellars became the ultimate in poor-quality housing, described by Shimmin as 'dingy ... and damp' (Shimmin 1862, 132). There was a campaign to reduce the frequency of cellar living. In 1850 Duncan recorded the benefit of the reduction of cellar dwelling to mortality rates:

> Liverpool affords a striking illustration of the beneficial effect of another important sanitary measure, namely, the abolishing of cellar habitations, and sending people to inhabit the surface of the earth, as they were intended to do ... In a certain district of the town before the fever of 1847 the cellar population amounted to about 12 per cent. of the entire population, and the fever carried off upwards of 500 of the inhabitants of the district. When the closely allied epidemic of cholera appeared, the inhabitants of the cellars in the same district had been reduced to 2 per cent. of the entire population, and deaths from cholera were only 94. (General Board of Health 1850, 114)

The excavated court housing in Oakes Street was found to have a cellar, accessed internally and used domestically with internal plaster on the walls. Its windows had been bricked up. The light wells to the windows were filled with domestic waste, which could be dated to between the 1880s and 1930s. The finds included glass bottles, pottery, leather shoes and boots, and even a 'dummy egg' used to encourage chickens to lay and to deter them from eating the eggs laid in the coop. A photograph of 1935, probably shortly before the demolition of the buildings, shows the light wells filled in.

Shimmin commended the action of some landlords in sealing up the cellars to prevent people trying to live in them, children from playing in them, or accidents when people fell down the steps into them. He

William Henry Duncan (1805–63)

Dr William Henry Duncan spearheaded public health campaigning around housing in the mid-nineteenth century, and especially focused on cellars. Having visited cellars, Duncan published his experiences, notably in his 1843 *On the Physical Causes of the High Rate of Mortality in Liverpool*. Although born in Liverpool, Duncan was of Scottish descent, and was educated in Scotland, graduating from Edinburgh University in 1829 (Halliday 2003, 142–9). He then returned to Liverpool, and worked as a general practitioner. His work brought him into contact with people from Liverpool's poorest areas, and Duncan started to record and research what he saw.

While working as a lecturer in the Royal Infirmary School of Medicine, Duncan presented papers and published reports recording the terrible conditions of court life, and demonstrating that most of the working-class population of the town was without sewers or piped water. *On the Physical Causes of the High Rate of Mortality in Liverpool* is a detailed review of the factors influencing health. In 1846 the first legislative attempts to improve housing conditions and prevent disease were enshrined in the Liverpool Sanitary Act. This gave responsibility for court cleansing to the corporation (Taylor 1970, 85–6). It also facilitated the creation of a new post, Medical Officer of Health, a role to which Duncan was appointed. In his then internationally unique role as a public health officer, Duncan campaigned against cellar dwelling, declaring 5,000 cellars unfit for human habitation in 1847 alone (Farrer and Brownbill 1966, 39).

Duncan's research frequently focused on housing as a factor in poor public health. Some of his early writing contained moralistic and judgmental comments, especially about Irish immigrants to Liverpool (Kearns et al. 1993, 96). Later his work made recommendations for improvements, through the law, which improved the urban environment.

cites the example of Duggan's Buildings (Walton and Wilcox 1991, 119). However, the campaigns to rid Liverpool of cellar homes were not completely successful in the nineteenth century. The proportion of the population living in cellars fell through the mid-nineteenth century, but in 1934 the *Social Survey of Merseyside* found at least 100 families still living in cellars (Caradog-Jones 1934).

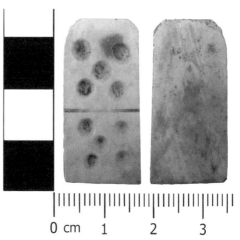

'The houses in general are in a dilapidated state, with broken doors, mouldering walls tumbling to ruin, broken windows'

5

Who lived in the courts?

Court housing provided relatively cheap accommodation for people in Liverpool from the eighteenth to the twentieth centuries. Some became 'slum' housing, but it was not always poor quality, and research suggests that residents came from a variety of backgrounds and undertook a wide range of types of work. Court houses were built in relatively uniform layouts, but were not consistent in their quality, maintenance, or the standard of living they offered.

Contemporary writers usually highlighted the worst-quality housing as part of the campaign for better housing and improvements in public health. 'The houses in general are in a dilapidated state, with broken doors, mouldering walls tumbling to ruin, broken windows, in some cases no windows at all, and some without fireplaces' (Finch 1833). Perhaps basing their articles on the famous writings of Engels, journalists reported on Leeds, Liverpool and Manchester 'slums'. In 1849 the *Morning Chronicle* described cellar homes in Leeds as 'wretched dwellings … inhabited by the Irish and the lowest class of English labourers, male and female' (*Morning Chronicle*, 13 December 1849, 3).

Contemporary descriptions of court housing often illustrate the terrible conditions in which people were living, and make difficult reading. Some look to explain people living in poor-quality housing by blaming their own failings – drunkenness, laziness or immorality. Some sources use racist, sexist and judgmental language. Shimmin's descriptions, for example, use anthropological phrases such as 'the whole colony which you find in this street', and he describes what he sees as 'instructive as to how people live' (*Porcupine*, 24 January 1863, 340–1).

Narrow court off Upper Stanhope Street, 1934
© Liverpool Record Office, Liverpool Libraries

Irish housing

Court housing is sometimes thought synonymous with Irish immigrants to Victorian Liverpool. In Liverpool a majority of the new immigrants from outside Lancashire in the mid-nineteenth century lived in courts, cellars or other forms of 'slum' housing. Censuses show some courts to have been entirely Irish areas (Belchem 2000, 151), but court and cellar housing in Liverpool was by no means exclusive to first-generation Irish migrants and refugees. While a majority of Irish people lived in courts, courts were not primarily home to solely Irish communities. Rather, census returns show people from Liverpool, Lancashire and elsewhere in England, Wales and Scotland, as well as Ireland, making courtyards the gathering spaces for mixed communities.

Liverpool's population increased rapidly in the nineteenth century as a result of inward migration and natural increase, with over 60% of adults in Britain in the 1870s having more than five children (Burnett 1978, 102). Migration into Liverpool in the early nineteenth century was most likely to be from north-west England and Wales, and then by the mid-nineteenth century from Ireland: 'occasioned by a scarcity of provision, bad bread, bad water and the state of Ireland causing numbers to flock to Liverpool in such distressed state that a violent dysentery ensued, followed by numerous deaths' (Smithers 1825, 199). Contemporary descriptions of Irish people show xenophobic contempt for them:

> Among the cases of fever in Liverpool, I might have enumerated the large proportion of poor Irish among the working population. It is they who inhabit the filthiest and worst-ventilated courts and cellars, who congregate the most numerously in dirty lodging-houses, who are the least cleanly in their habits. (Duncan 1842, 293–4)

Similarly, Friedrich Engels wrote of Irish lifestyles, presumably reflecting views he had heard while visiting Britain: 'These [Irish] people having grown up almost without civilisation, accustomed from youth to every sort of privation, rough, intemperate, and improvident, [and] bring all their brutal habits with them' (Engels 1845, 90). Peak immigration was in the mid-1840s, largely as a result of the Great Hunger in Ireland. Between January and April 1847 127,850 Irish people arrived in Liverpool (Miller 1988, 13). By 1851 49.4% of Liverpool's population had been born outside Lancashire. While the mixture of these populations has created a unique culture in Liverpool (Belchem 2007), the arrival of large numbers of new people in the early Victorian period created a demand for cheap housing. Some areas were quickly being informally demarcated for different communities. The rapid construction of poor-quality housing for growing communities became a profitable enterprise (Miller 1988, 13; Pooley 1977, 372; Pooley 1984, 136). The living conditions of Irish people in Liverpool attracted particular comment in contemporary descriptions, including by public health professionals: 'the number of poor especially of Irish and other destitute immigrants promiscuously collected in certain squalid localities' (Trench 1865, 7).

Census data shows the proportions of Liverpool-born people and those moving to the town from elsewhere living in courts. The census information for the last extant remains of court housing in Liverpool, on Pembroke Place, has been investigated in detail.

It has been found, for example, that in 1851 80% of the residents of Watkinson's Buildings were not born in Lancashire. They were from Cheshire, the Isle of Man, Wales, Shropshire, Yorkshire, Cumberland, Northumberland and Scotland, but interestingly not Ireland (Beastall 2017, 4).

An assumed link between the Irish community and the poorest-quality housing was also repeatedly stated in nineteenth-century descriptions of Manchester, but census data does not support this presumption. Hayton's work on Manchester and Rochdale cellar dwellings, and the archaeological work undertaken through the Alderley Sandhills and Dig Manchester project, has started to explore the materiality of workers' housing in urban and semi-rural areas of Greater Manchester. Hayton uses census data to demonstrate that cellars were not uniquely Irish as contemporary writers assert, instead showing a mixing of the Irish into the existing populations, with little discrepancy between levels of overcrowding in Irish and non-Irish homes, and little difference in occupational patterns between the two groups. So while potential sectarian or political divisions may be difficult to trace, historical sources demonstrate mixing of communities (Hayton 1998, 66–77).

The economics of court housing

Court housing was among the cheapest types of housing to construct, and commanded the lowest rents. It was found across Liverpool, and accommodated people working in many industries. 'Slum' housing was not closely associated with dock industries; indeed, 'sailortown' areas benefited from the residents being likely to be in frequent employment (Milne 2016, 65). Dock labour was notoriously casual, workers responding to arriving ships, and undertaking unloading, carting and support work. The density of population in courts varied, and they were most likely to be overcrowded in central areas and nearer the docks, where properties could accommodate families and were also sometimes sub-let to lodgers.

Some living conditions in courts were horrifyingly overcrowded, insanitary and damp.

> The present augmentation of individuals in each dwelling clearly arises from the numbers of small houses now being sufficiently proportioned to the increase in the mediocrity, which increase must be undoubtedly very unhealthy to inhabitants ... Many hundreds [of houses] which do not rent for four to six pounds per annum have eighteen

to twenty crowded together from cellar to garret under one roof. (Wallace 1797, 70)

Some courts seem to have been slightly higher quality, with professional residents living respectable lives in small but well-kept homes. Higher-quality houses were occasionally noted in the nineteenth century; for example, Hugh Shimmin describes Hughes Cottages: 'There are four houses in the court, and all are fancifully, if not artistically decorated, Green window shutters, yellow window sills, and red steps edged with white! ... the whole of the houses are remarkably clean' (Shimmin 1862, 110). Shimmin's comments were aimed at demonstrating that it was the inhabitants rather than the homes which made court housing poor quality. He often relates the quality of life being lived in courts not to the buildings, but to the moral strength of the people: 'the home of the labourer, poor and unwholesome as it generally is, is not always a wretched one. Even in these dismal courts may be occasionally found a happy little home, brightened by a smart tidy little wife and a sober studious husband' (*Liverpool Mercury*, 25 December 1882, 6).

Excavation of Missionary Buildings on Oakes Street, Liverpool, revealed finds dumped in the coal chute and cellar window

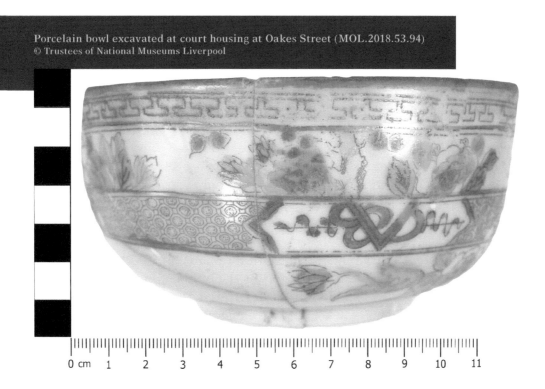

Porcelain bowl excavated at court housing at Oakes Street (MOL.2018.53.94) © Trustees of National Museums Liverpool

light wells after the cellar was put out of use. In the coal chute finds included a near-complete porcelain bowl. While it is not impossible that this had been brought from elsewhere, it is likely that it was in use nearby, and possibly in the court itself. This indicates some relatively high-quality belongings being used in the court. This archaeological evidence reinforces the picture that census information gives of very varied living conditions in the courts. Reviewing archaeological assemblages from workers' housing has suggested a variety of lifestyles and experiences (Crook 2011, 582–93). The 1861 census for Missionary Buildings (which later became known as Court 2, Oakes Street), reveals residents who were tailors, shoemakers, masons, a French polisher, a watchmaker, a midwife and a confectioner. These occupations were skilled, and demonstrate that people living in courts were not necessarily at the lowest end of the social spectrum (Stewart et al. forthcoming).

Some of the variation in the quality of the courts was reflected in the rents charged for the houses. Writing in his 'Liverpool Life' series in the late 1850s, Shimmin mentions some of the contemporary rents: 'The rents vary from 2s. 9d. to 4s. 6d., according to locality'. Shimmin's comments on the economics of court living show some sympathies for those of the tenants who were on low wages. Other examples refer to their lifestyles, especially drinking, as keeping them in poverty (Walton and Wilcox 1991, 108–9).

A detailed survey of 1907–08 captures household incomes and expenditure on rent for working-class people in Liverpool, primarily families in which the main income was from dock labour (Rathbone 1909). Averaging wages and rents for forty individuals, some surveyed just once, others recorded for over a year, this demonstrates that on average 21% of household income was being spent on rent. It also shows the variation in income from week to week, and the frequent necessity for some families to skip the rent and cut other costs, including food, in weeks when little had been earned.

Pressure on income from rent was noted in the nineteenth century: 'the dock labourer's home is a poor one. House-rent in Liverpool is high, much higher than in any town or city in England except London' (*Liverpool Mercury*, 25 December 1882, 6). This is supported by Troughton's assertion in 1810 of high rents in Liverpool due to inward migration from Ireland and increased demand: 'In the summer of 1798, so great was the influx of persons of every description into this town, from Ireland, that house rent, and the price of lodgings were greatly advanced' (Troughton 1810, 198).

Sense of community

People arriving in Liverpool often settled themselves into the communal life of a court, predominantly run by women. Hugh Shimmin described how one woman moving in to a court was visited by her new neighbours as she and her family unpacked: 'One wanted to wish her good luck; some wanted to borrow pans and mugs; some wished her to join them in a subscription to bury a child that was dead in the top house' (Walton and Wilcox 1991, 156). While the low-cost court and cellar housing available in Liverpool would have attracted many people newly arrived for short-term rentals, censuses also show courts to have been long-term homes for families, with occasional cases of multiple generations of a family living in one court, and people staying in a court for two censuses. At Burlington Street, the Hughes family lived in Albert Terrace court in 1871, and were still there in 1881. In fact, John, the elder son of Thomas and Elizabeth Hughes, moved in to another house in the court when he was married. Families might have been informally encouraged to stay in their court, as there was a concern that people moving around frequently increased the spread of disease: 'frequent changes of residence, scattering and resewing thereby the seeds of infectious diseases, the crowding together of many families in single houses' (Trench 1865, 7).

In a city where people would have mingled daily in the streets, at work, while shopping, and in pubs or cocoa rooms, it is highly unlikely that people regularly moving home would have had a real impact on disease and mortality rates.

The neighbourly communal spirit would have been enhanced by shared experience, and there is some evidence in censuses that people working in the same trades lived together, although it cannot be known whether work colleagues shared information on vacant homes or neighbours shared information about work opportunities.

> It's just my opinion like but … it's about people not places. And the more people, everybody was packed in, and you learnt something from everybody, so all those people you could virtually say that it was a mass of opinions and skills, helping you to judge things. That was the good part of living in a packed area where people found it hard to live. (Rich Lyon, on living in a court in the 1930s and 1940s, Museum of Liverpool oral history collection)

There is some evidence that the arrangement of private dwellings around a communal open space was a housing type that fostered a communal spirit. When asked why they did not leave the court and seek out better housing, court residents told Hugh Shimmin that they had

Groups of people stand outside court houses at Mount Vernon View in 1935
© Liverpool Record Office, Liverpool Libraries

friends and neighbours there, and that 'a neighbour was not to be met with in any place or any day', explaining it would be hard to leave the people who had shared happiness and sorrow over the years (Walton and Wilcox 1991, 116). From an economic point of view, court housing may have been more desirable for its location in relation to work, and its proximity to family, friends and colleagues, than for the cheapness of the rent (Pooley 1977, 372; Pooley 1984, 136).

It is difficult to assess, from historical documents, whether religious sectarianism, political ghettoization or other divisions were exacerbated by the physical structures of housing in discrete clusters. The dispersal of newly arrived groups such as Irish immigrants has been traced in Manchester (Hayton 1998, 66–77). This is also seen in Liverpool, suggesting that there was not always a strong pattern of communities living in distinct areas. Although there would have been some clustering of people with shared outlooks, there also seems, from the information recorded about people in nineteenth-century censuses, to have been significant mixing throughout the central 'core' areas of Liverpool.

Migrant communities tended to focus around services which developed for them in a core area of settlement, and churches especially were a key focus (Belchem 2000). People chose where not to live as well as where to live. Scottish churches on Oldham Street and Rodney Street sent an official to find out more about the housing of Scottish people in Liverpool, and John Turner concluded that 'Scottish habits and feelings render them exceedingly averse to a residence among the society which frequently congregate in the courts and back houses of the denser inhabited parts of the town' (Turner 1836, 15).

Ilhas, Oporto, Portugal

Houses around courtyards are found in a variety of contexts around the world. Some, like British court housing, have shared courtyards with shared facilities. These spaces often create communal spaces. While these can be valued by residents, they cause concern for society.

In Oporto, Portugal, the Ilhas were of a similar layout to British courts, and existed from the nineteenth to the twentieth centuries. In the growing port and industrial city, they provided accommodation for the increasing population. The Ilhas were dwellings arranged around a courtyard, with shared facilities: toilet, wash room and well. These were tight-knit communities sharing the semi-private space of the courtyard (Pereira 1994). However, historical records show concern about the social conditions in the Ilhas, referring to alcoholism, prostitution and crime as common among the inhabitants (Mata 1909).

6

Inside the courts

The many written records of court houses describe, from the point of view of health officials and journalists, what conditions were like:

> house after house, and we have found in so many cases literally nothing but the bare walls, a heap of straw covered by bare rags, and possibly the remains of a broken chair or table. In London, and every large town, such rooms may be found, but the peculiarity of Liverpool is, that they are so numerous. (Parkes and Sanderson 1871, 65)

There are descriptions of the form and layout of the buildings, many of which also describe something of how it felt to be in those spaces; cramped homes which were 'much too small, and almost throughout too low' (Moss 1784, 54). Written descriptions of court housing tend to present the most extreme interpretations of life in nineteenth-century Liverpool, intending to shock readers:

> In the back part of this house … there is a dwelling worthy of particular attention. It is the home of a father, mother and five children. The rooms they occupy are immediately over a stable and midden, and the privy, which is used in common is under the stairs. The entrance of the house is up a dark, crooked flight of stairs. You cannot walk straight going up, the ceiling is so low, and when you gain the first landing the stench from below is stifling. (Shimmin 1864, 11–12)

The layout of these buildings, and access to shared open space, would have defined some aspects of lifestyles and activity. There would have been less privacy than in modern homes, and everyday cooking, eating, washing, work and entertainment would not have been undertaken in separate spaces, but all in a ground-floor living room (Burnett 1978, 75). The outdoor space of the court would also have

functioned as a shared space for much domestic activity.

Life in courts would have been very varied, as is shown by sometimes contradictory descriptions. Asked about whether court houses were comfortable, one oral history participant recollected, 'you'd wake up in the morning and the frost would be on the inside of the window in the bedroom' (Kenneth Smith, on living in a court in Mann Street in the 1940s and 1950s, Museum of Liverpool oral history collection). Another individual describes a court in the same period, remembering 'the fire was on all the time. Even of a night it was on very, very low … you'd get it going again of a morning time, you know. The houses were always warm' (Bernard Rowan, on living in a court off Saltney Street in the 1940s and 1950s, Museum of Liverpool oral history collection).

Some memories show the consistent design of court houses. One oral history participant remembered,

> you came through the door to your lounge – if you could call it a lounge – it was one square 4 m x 3 m; it was twelve square metres, at the most. From your door you had your staircase; the staircase went up to the first floor; then went round and went to the second floor, which was three small rooms. (Angela Rooney, on living in court housing in Johnson Terrace in the 1940s and 1950s, Museum of Liverpool oral history collection)

Another oral history records,

> starting from the base there was a cellar … steps going up so there was a front room and a back room. Now they weren't very big, I'd say they were roughly 12 ft x 12 ft … there was stairs going upstairs to the next level … there was two rooms because I had a sister who was in one and I shared the other one with my cousin who came with live with us. (Rich Lyon, on living in a court in the 1930s and 1940s, Museum of Liverpool oral history collection)

Written descriptions from the nineteenth century and oral histories from the twentieth century consistently note the limited amount of furniture: 'in those days people never used to have anything to store [laugh]' (Rich Lyon, on living in a court in the 1930s and 1940s, Museum of Liverpool oral history collection). Written descriptions suggest that for some people the situation didn't change substantially decade-to-decade. 'His furniture is simple and primitive. A round table with three legs, two or three chairs, of various build and design, a couple of stools, a dresser for the few plates and dishes required, and a few soiled prints on the wall' (*Liverpool Mercury*, 25 December 1882, 6).

Such written and oral histories are vital in understanding life in court housing as few interior photographs were taken.

‘It is they who inhabit the filthiest and worst-ventilated courts and cellars, who congregate the most numerously in dirty lodging-houses, who are the least cleanly in their habits.’

Abraham Hume (1814–84)

There were people in Liverpool with political and social power who worked to improve the housing and lives of working-class people. In attempts to initiate improvements in housing conditions, philanthropists and social reformers had been mapping Liverpool's urban poor since the mid-nineteenth century.

The Revd Abraham Hume was a vicar in the Church of England, who worked as a curate in Liverpool before being appointed vicar of the new parish of Vauxhall. In Vauxhall he undertook considerable research into the people of his parish. He mapped the 'pauper streets', where 'the poor crowd themselves upon the spots gradually deserted by the rich' (Hume 1858, 20). He identified concentrations of poor people living near the docks in the north and south of the town (Hume 1858, 22). This distribution, he found, reflected the importance of the docks in the employment of many of the residents of the courts, directly or indirectly. As the poor state of court houses became more commonly understood, legislation and other action was brought into force to improve the lives of people living in the poorest housing.

'Outstanding defects
[of court housing] were
its lack of proper
amenities – almost
certainly no piped
water-supply
to each house'

7

Sanitation and health in court housing

Liverpool was stigmatized from the mid-nineteenth century as the 'most unhealthy town in England' (Treble 1971, 168). In 1838 Liverpool had the highest rate of mortality in Britain (Miller 1988, 11). Average age at death for labourers, mechanics and servants in Liverpool was found to be 15, and 35 for gentry and professional persons (Duncan 1843, 63). Very high child mortality rates contributed to these horrendous statistics. The economy of the town had adapted to insecure, low-wage dock work, including the provision of cheap and poor-quality housing (Duncan 1843, 62–5). It was quickly recognized that the housing was contributing to the poor health of the population. The high density of poorer people living in insanitary conditions led to bad health, and outbreaks of disease.

> The unfavourable conditions of the residence of the working classes will, of course, be felt most readily and most severely by those of feeble constitutions, where the powers of nature are unable to wage an unequal war with such a numerous cohort of morbific agencies. (Duncan 1843, 30–1)

Many of the nineteenth-century records of court housing relate to public health concerns. Liverpool Corporation (predecessor of the City Council) sought to improve conditions by passing the 1846 Liverpool Sanitary Act. This supported the posts of Medical Officer of Health, Borough Engineer and Inspector of Nuisances. James Newlands was appointed as Borough Engineer in 1847, and immediately started mapping and recording the situation, and planning for a new water-based sewerage system. By 1869 three hundred miles of sewers had been constructed to serve the houses of Liverpool.

In the mid-nineteenth century the spread of disease was often attributed to 'miasma', unhealthy vapours in the air. Unhealthy places were associated with foul odours, and those were considered to be what carried the illnesses. Miasma theories were clearly incorrect, but did lead public health officials and campaigners to improve sewerage and ventilation, work towards better treatment of refuse, and act against damp properties (Halliday 2001, 1469–71).

Duncan's writings subscribe to the notion of 'human miasma' (Kearns et al. 1993, 98). He frequently refers to overcrowding and lack of fresh air as a contributing factor in illness, including outbreaks of highly contagious diseases such as cholera. 'Such an arrangement almost bids defiance to the entrance of air, and renders its free circulation throughout the court a matter of impossibility' (Duncan 1843, 10). James Newlands, who worked alongside Duncan to devise engineering solutions to sewerage and fresh water supply, also attributed the spread of disease to the miasma hypothesis:

> Dense masses crowded in small space generate miasmas hungry for life, which grow with what they feed upon. It is proved beyond question that increase of density when population is the same in other respects, is followed by increases in mortality. How necessary it is then to endeavour to secure by structural arrangements that amount of space for every individual which health demands. (Newlands 1848, 106)

When public health officials, social reformers and journalists visited courts from the 1840s they identified numerous problems which made life unpleasant and insanitary. As well as lack of ventilation, they frequently cited overcrowding, lack of fresh water supply and sewerage, lack of light, damp, the poor quality of the buildings, and the lack of furniture and furnishings.

> With regard to their dwellings, I would point out as the principal circumstances affecting the health of the poor:
>
> 1. Imperfect ventilation.
>
> 2. Want of places of deposit for vegetable and animal refuse.
>
> 3. Imperfect drainage and sewerage.
>
> 4. Imperfect system of scavenging and cleansing.
>
> The circumstances derived from their habits most prejudicial to their health, I conceive to be:

1. Their tendency to congregate in too large numbers under the same roof, &c.

2. Want of cleanliness.

3. Indisposition to be removed to the hospital when ill of fever. (Poor Law Commissioners 1842, 283–4)

Early courts were built without sewerage or running water. At the time of construction many courts were not provided with their own water pipes. Instead, water had to be collected from a standpipe in the street. Samuel Holmes, a Liverpool builder, told the State of Large Towns Enquiry in 1844: 'Generally a court containing

A woman collects water from a standpipe in a court in Saltney Street, 1906
© Liverpool Record Office, Liverpool Libraries

Girls photographed in a court off Rathbone Street with privies in the background
© Liverpool Record Office, Liverpool Libraries

16 houses will have two single privies, for the accommodation of a population averaging 80 persons' (Commissioners for Inquiring into the State of Large Towns and Populous Districts 1844). From the 1850s water standpipes started to be installed in courts, but this was by no means universal. 'There was no water at all in the house. I don't know how we did it, but we had to do all the washing outside' (McKenna, quoted in Pooley, 2000, 449).

In the late eighteenth century the city surveyors recognized that the sewerage system was inadequate, but the problem was not remedied. Instead temporary arrangements were made to deal with specific problems; for example in 1787, 'Ordered that Mr Eyes do immediately take every necessary measure in order to prevent the water in future incommoding the tenants of the houses in Paradise Street, by flowing into the cellars on the occasion of the fall of rain' (Picton 1886, 260). As the population grew the corporation found it hard to cope with the growth in demand for water supply, sewerage and public health, refuse and street cleaning, and facilities for recreation (Simey 1951, 5). These problems only started to become clear to the politicians and the middle- and upper-class people of Liverpool when journalists and public health officials started to visit the courts, and their experiences were made public. The research undertaken by Duncan and others revealed the scale of the problem: 'a population whose solid excretions alone ... must amount to between two and three hundred thousand pounds weekly, or nearly six thousand tons annually' (Duncan 1843, 12). 'The fluid contents ... spread a layer of abomination over the entire surface of the court. In some instances it even oozes through into the neighbouring cellars' (Duncan 1843, 13). And the shortcomings of the existing arrangements were clear: 'Ash pits generally become full to overflowing, long before the nightmen make their appearance to empty them' (Duncan 1843, 13).

The excavated example of a Liverpool court on Oakes Street revealed a brick sewer, approximately 1.4 metres beneath the courtyard level. This had probably been constructed contemporaneously with the second section of court homes, which seem from map evidence to have been built in two phases, the west range by 1830 and the east range between 1835 and 1847. The sewer ran along the centre of the courtyard parallel with the houses, and was topped by a brick arch (Stewart et al. forthcoming). The sewer was not fully excavated because of its depth and accessibility in the trench.

While the infrastructure of sewerage and water supply was slow to be addressed, the Sanitary Act

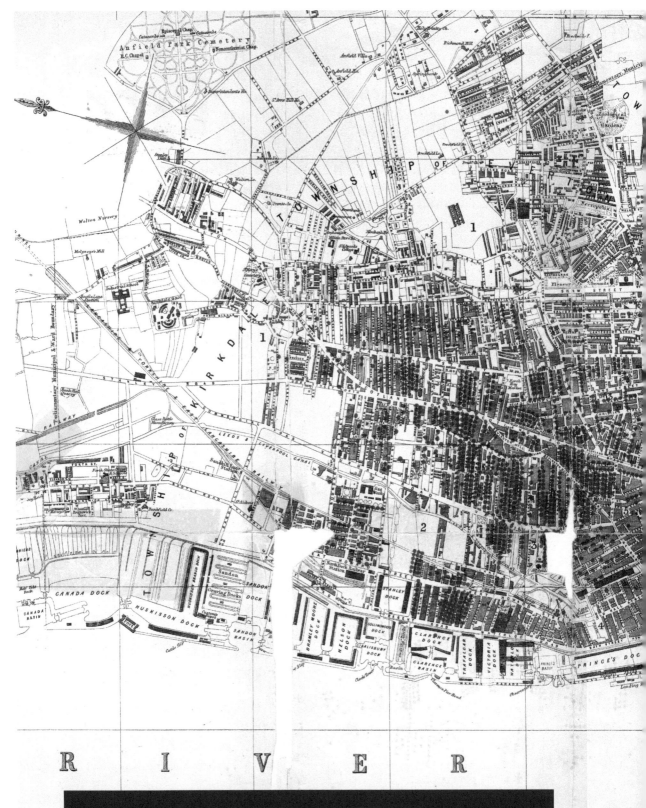

Cholera map of 1866, showing cases of the disease clustering along streets
where there was court housing
© Liverpool Record Office, Liverpool Libraries

BOROUGH of LIVERPOOL
MORTALITY MAP OF CHOLERA
In 1866.

The Red Dots mark the number of Deaths.

SCALE OF ½ MILE

REFERENCE TO THE WARDS —

1 Everton & Kirkdale
2 Scotland
3 Vauxhall
4 St Paul's
5 Exchange
6 Castle Street
7 St Peter's
8 Pitt Street
9 Great George
10 Rodney Street
11 Abercromby
12 Lime Street
13 St Anne's Street
14 West Derby
15 South Toxteth
16 North Toxteth

In addition to the circles which mark death from Cholera, there should be added the following, now left out from want of space, viz :—

Milton Street 22
Back Milton Street . . 2
Harrison Street . . . 5
Back Portland Street . 2
Kew Street 5

NOTE, THE RED CROSSES MARK THE SITUATION OF THE ASHFIELD STREET
LIVERPOOL WORKHOUSE & EVERTON TERRACE CHOLERA HOSPITALS.

1846 demanded that the corporation take responsibility for the cleansing and sanitation of the courts. It also provided for the appointment of Duncan as Medical Officer for Health. Duncan had recorded a few years earlier that

> In the streets inhabited by the working classes, I believe that the great majority are without sewers, and that where they do exist they are of a very imperfect kind unless where the ground has a natural inclination, therefore the surface water and fluid refuse of every kind stagnate in the street, and add, especially in hot weather, their pestilential influence to that of the more solid filth. With regard to the courts, I doubt whether there is a single court in Liverpool which communicates with the street by an underground drain, the only means afforded for carrying off the fluid dirt being a narrow, open, shallow gutter, which sometimes exists, but even this is very generally choked up with stagnant filth. (Duncan 1842, 287–8)

In 1844 a Liverpool builder is quoted as lamenting the lack of proper drainage in Liverpool's courts:

> there are thousands of houses and hundreds of courts ... without a single drain of any description, and I never hail anything with greater delight than I do a violent tempest or a terrific thunderstorm accompanied by heavy rain, for these are the only scavengers that thousands have to cleanse away impurities and the filth in which they live or, rather, exist. (Beames 1852, 173)

Public health officials were keen to show the effect of improvements.

> As an instance of the benefit derived from sanitary improvements – I may mention Lace-street, which, as you know, was formerly one of the most unhealthy streets in Liverpool. In 1847 it was undrained; and in that year about 200 deaths from fever occurred in the street, in addition to about 250 from other causes. About the end of 1848 it was sewered; and during the epidemic of the following year [1849] the deaths from cholera were only 36. (General Board of Health 1850, 113–14)

Cholera was a serious cause for concern in the mid-nineteenth century. Outbreaks of the disease struck Liverpool in 1832, 1848–49, 1854 and 1866. The 1832 outbreak caused riots as people feared its spread and found the medical and political responses to it 'variable and inadequate' (Burrell and Gill 2005, 478). The sudden outbreaks had immediate and drastic effects on individuals, families and court communities. The 1849 epidemic, for example, claimed 6,394 lives in Liverpool (Miller 1988, 13). However, it was the ongoing impact of other diseases which caused the greater toll of fatalities overall. Tuberculosis, typhus and typhoid, diarrhoea, dysentery, diphtheria, measles, whooping cough and scarlet fever tended to be concentrated in the poor, densely built housing with the worst sanitation, though other parts of the city were certainly also subject to the widespread impact of these diseases (Pooley 2006, 225).

Public officials identified the need to improve services:

> In my Report to the Health Committee in 1848 I advocated the introduction of water closets to courts and small dwellings, but remarked that the closet should be adapted to the place it is to occupy and to the habits of the users. I there described a kind of closet adapted for back yards, courts, and public necessaries. These have been largely introduced into public institutions, schools, &c., and an experience of their working of nearly sixteen years' duration warrants the conclusion that they admirably serve their purpose. (Newlands 1863, 35)

Indeed, it was the supply of clean water and the taking away of waste that was the key to improved health. In 1855 the ability of cholera to be transmitted through water was observed by Dr Snow of London, and the causal agent of that process was discovered in 1883. William Budd's studies in 1856 established the presence of faeces as a factor in the spread of typhoid fever (Moorhead 2002). Towns sought to control their water supplies, wresting back control from private companies which had moved into that area in the 1830s and 1840s (Sheard 1993, 141). Water supplies were controlled, and water could be switched on for short periods. Some homes used this time to allow cisterns to be filled, but where there were no cisterns people had to improvise with containers (Sheard 1993, 148).

> [O]utstanding defects [of court housing] were its lack of proper amenities – almost certainly no piped water-supply to each house, except in Nottingham ... shared neglected privy at some distance from the house, the lack of adequate services for refuse removal ... And even where communal wash-houses were provided, the absence of open ground to hang out washing to dry, necessitating the use of lines across dirty streets. (Burnett 1978, 75)

By the 1860s the health of Liverpool's children in particular was a cause for great concern: 'In relation to epidemic and intestinal diseases, Liverpool's mortality was one-and-a-half times the national rate and chest diseases were 60 per cent higher' (Lawton and Lee 2002, 108). Both were reflected in very high child and infant mortality, which accounted for 40–60% of deaths in the mid-Victorian period. 'Of the deaths which occurred amongst the labouring classes in Liverpool, it appears that no less than 62% of the total number were deaths under five years of age. Even amongst those entered as shopkeepers and tradesmen, no less than 50% died before they attained that period' (Chadwick 1842, 159). These terrible statistics led to the establishment of hospitals, especially in the pavilion style, with light airy wards (Miller 1988, 31; Carpenter 2010, 31). Liverpool had had an infirmary since 1745, and in response to the growing population the Northern Hospital was opened in 1834, moving to larger, purpose-built premises in 1845. However, throughout the Victorian period it proved harder for the corporation to deal with the major cause of some of the illnesses, namely the housing in which people were living.

By 1863 James Newlands was able to report that over 58 miles of sewers had been built to serve the housing of the town, as well as 30 miles of courts and passage drains (Newlands 1863, 4). This doubled the rate of sewer building from that seen over the previous decade.

Contemporary writing about court life continued to focus on the poor conditions, part of an ongoing campaign for more legislation, investment and other action to improve the living conditions of Liverpool's poorest people. The cleanliness of courts was a point of comment for public health officers, such as Edward Hope: 'The court is fairly good. The house is very dirty; it has 3 rooms, 2 of which only contain packs and straw (dirty) for bedding. Food consists of bread with mussels + similar maritime vermin' (Hope 1883–88, 8). Legal action was sometimes taken to order courts to be cleaned and conditions improved, for example in 1865: 'No 6 Court Pembroke street … surrounded with deposits and refuse, &c. The bench issued an order for the closing of the premises; but it was understood that if Mr Makinson would make the house fit for use the order would be rescinded' (*Liverpool Mercury*, 2 February 1865, 7).

Enhanced legislative controls gradually came into force, aimed at stemming the spread of disease by improving conditions. The 1866 Public Health Act amended the 1865

Sewage Utilisation Act, providing for better drainage from houses.

Quality of buildings

Court housing tended to follow a fairly consistent plan form, on different scales, from two houses to over a dozen in a court. The build quality of these houses seems to have varied considerably, however. Contemporary commentators noted this variation:

> There are in Liverpool many courts constructed on a good plan having back yards and conveniences to each house, and a passage between the back yards of the contiguous courts. These courts are commonly open at both ends, which gives a proper circulation of air, and, being flagged, they are easily kept clean. Such places, when they do not consist of more than six or eight houses, are, apart from the vital error of over-crowding, tolerably healthy, and are in general, inhabited by an industrious and cleanly description of tenants. (Newlands 1863, 25)

The materials used for the houses themselves were blamed for the spread of disease:

> second hand bricks from sites of demolished insanitary houses owned by the corporation have

been used in houses now in the course of erection ... There is a considerable divergence of opinion as to the chance of survival of bugs in infested bricks ... when an infested brick is well embedded in mortar and its internal surface is covered in plaster, it is impossible for the insects to escape into the house. (Health Committee 1936, 1101–07)

Contemporary commentators placed much responsibility on the tenants for the cleanliness and condition of their homes: 'Some courts in back Grafton street showed clearly, by the neat manner in which they were kept, how much depends upon the tenants for keeping houses decent' (Shimmin 1862, 108). It was women who were specifically expected to control their living conditions: 'whenever you found a clean house, or a cleanly kept court, you found a clean wife and clean children' (Shimmin 1862, 109).

Shimmin describes some court houses which may have been decently built, but which had been badly maintained and were in a terrible state of repair, with pigeons in the roofspace, windows with broken or missing glass, and broken steps and flags. Some of the damage was clearly directly linked to poverty, such as skirting boards being removed for firewood (Walton and Wilcox 1991, 116).

The extant remains of court

Brick-built court houses off Falkner Street, lime-washed to control disease and reflect light
© Liverpool Record Office, Liverpool Libraries

housing which have been investigated show this variation in build quality, even in closely juxtaposed geographical areas. 35–39 Pembroke Place is the last surviving court housing in Liverpool. These buildings incorporate

the truncated remains of two courts, Watkinson's Buildings and Watkinson's Terrace, originally courts containing eight houses each. The three remaining houses have now been converted into storerooms for shops. These buildings were constructed in the early 1840s, and are reasonably solidly constructed of even brickwork with bricks which have not badly degraded. There is some architectural detailing, including brick arches above the front doors. The block behind the Pembroke Place courts was another court, accessed from Oakes Street. This court, excavated in 2018, was found not to be well constructed. Internal walls are badly bonded, and external features that were apparently part of the original design, such as the coal cellar and window light wells, are not bonded into the front wall (Stewart et al. forthcoming).

Inside this last extant example of court housing in Liverpool it is evident how small the rooms of these homes were, less than 3.5 metres wide and the same deep, and originally accommodating a staircase in that space. The size of court housing was recorded by public health officers. The early courts of Liverpool were entered through very narrow passageways, and many of the courtyards were narrow, just 10–15 feet wide (Burnett 1978, 72). 'In the North division of the Parish of Liverpool, there are 673 courts which have entrances of 3 feet wide or under' (Newlands 1863, 25–6).

In contemporary assessments probably the greatest problem of court housing was considered to be that 'no breath of air can reach the unhappy residents which is not fraught with offensive and deleterious compounds' (Trench 1863, 6). In the context of miasma theory and concern about 'bad air', the lack of ventilation in courts constructed before the 1840s was of great concern for public health: 'many deplorable cases of general ill health and mortality in such places, attributed at first to deficiency or bad quality of food, or to any cause but the true one – want of ventilation' (Duncan 1843, 32). 'In small pent-up areas, where the means of ventilation are denied ... there can be little doubt as to its being an efficient cause of fever, the fact being established by nearly every medical writer of repute' (Duncan 1843, 21). 'Abundance of air in motion or ventilation is also essential to health, not only of the body but also the mind. Thus it seems that space, light and ventilation are essentials of health' (Newlands 1848, 106). It was thought that life in this type of housing could soon descend into 'nurseries of disease' (Trench 1863, 8). A solution for dark and ill-ventilated court housing was the introduction of 'open courts' – where the courtyard opened straight on to the street, rather than access being through an arched passageway between street-front buildings.

In the 1890s and 1900s, Dr Darra Mair investigated sanitary conditions and reported to local

House in Watkinson's Terrace,
photographed in 2016
© Trustees of National Museums Liverpool

government officials across the UK. He considered mortality rates in back-to-back housing across England in 1908–09, and even at this late date his conclusions highlighted the insanitary nature of the dark, airless homes (Darra Mair 1910).

Commentators were concerned about the lack of light in courts and court houses. Due to their being built back-to-back, and therefore only having one window on one elevation on each floor, itself opening on to an often shaded courtyard, there was limited light into these homes: 'the importance of light as a sanitary agent is universally admitted. It is the hand maid of cleanliness; darkness and dirtiness are commonly convertible terms. The want of it engenders idleness and habits of filth too often accompanied by moral depravity' (Newlands 1848, 106). The problem of courts being built in the shadow of large warehouses or factories was a growing concern as industrial Victorian Liverpool developed larger buildings. By the late nineteenth century there was considerable comment on the physical condition of courts, often linked to their moral condition:

> A great deal of immorality was created and fostered by our dark courts. We therefore undertook to light up a few of them … this brought about a burst of indignation from the poor people … the lighting up of the Courts

being a novel thing, many of the children played about and made a great noise. (Postance 1884, 8)

Despite the complaints of the residents, the corporation continued this 'experiment', and gas lighting was brought into the courts, often featuring in early twentieth-century photographs.

A further problem with the poor-quality construction of some court housing was damp, and this was a particular issue with inhabited cellars. The Health of Town Committee undertook a survey in 1844 which showed that in the Vauxhall area of Liverpool, 36% of the inhabited cellars were classified as 'damp', while 2.4% were 'wet' (Health of Town Committee 1846). The situation in the Pitt Street area was worse, with 66% of cellars there being damp and 3.5% wet (Dennis 1984, 62). This problem had been identified as early as the eighteenth century, when there were reports of cellars flooding when it rained (Taylor 1970, 4–5).

Access to light and air was eventually improved through legislation, and damp cellars were put out of use and infilled. However, the overall standard of living in Liverpool court housing remained low into the twentieth century. From the early twentieth century living standards and the policies which created them were compared internationally, sometimes reflecting

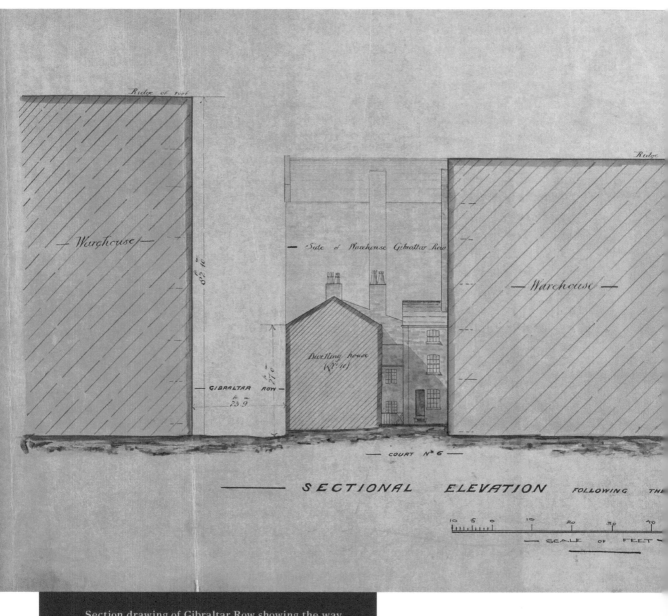

Ridge of roof

— Warehouse —

82 10

— Side of Warehouse Gibraltar Row

— Warehouse —

Ridge

Dwelling house
(N°. 10)

GIBRALTAR ROW
23 9

21 0

— COURT N° 6 —

——— SECTIONAL ELEVATION FOLLOWING THE

10 5 0 10 20 30 40

— SCALE OF FEET —

Section drawing of Gibraltar Row showing the way
in which adjacent warehouses overshadow houses in
courts, making the space dark
© Liverpool Record Office, Liverpool Libraries

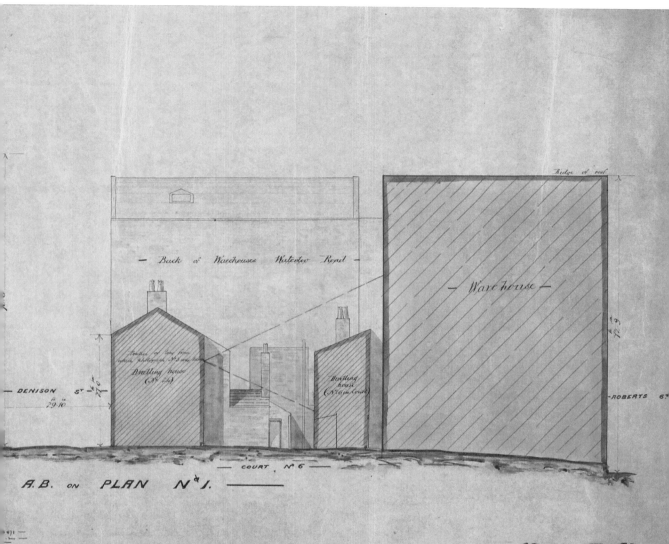

— Back of Warehouse Waterloo Road —

— Warehouse —

ridge of roof

Dwelling house
(N° 24)

Dwelling
house
(N° 6 in Court)

DENISON ST.

ROBERTS ST.

— COURT N° 6 —

A.B. ON PLAN N° 1. ————————

LP 2013

how far conditions had been improved. On a visit to New York in 1910 Professor Adshead, director of the Department of Civic Design at the University of Liverpool, told the New York Mayor's Commission on the Congestion of Population,

I am afraid that in the matter of admitted requirement as regards light and air in England and Germany, there is no question that the standard set by New York is infinitely too low … my impression is that the occupants cannot be described as poor. They are exceedingly well dressed, well fed and clean in their persons. When compared with

Damp was rife in many courts, and especially cellar dwellings, into the twentieth century
© Liverpool Record Office, Liverpool Libraries

the slum-dwellers in England the cleanliness and tidiness of their rooms are beyond all question superior. (Adshead 1910, 11)

Uncleanliness and the spread of disease

In 1748 the first Act was sought by the corporation to ensure the cleanliness of the town, 'for the enlightening and cleansing of the streets of the said town, and for keeping and maintaining a nightly watch there' (House of Commons 1803, 641). As the population grew, and the sewerage and services provided failed to keep pace, the level of disease in Liverpool rose. In the late eighteenth century Liverpool was a thriving port town, but still with a manageable population of around 50,000. In this period, the historian Enfield recorded the current situation, finding mortality rates to be 36.7 per 1,000, but stated that Liverpool 'may with confidence be pronounced a healthful place' (Enfield 1773, 29). Fifty years later another researcher, Smithers, used burial rates to compare mortality rates around the UK, and concluded that the proportion of the population

dying in Liverpool was the highest in Britain (Smithers 1825, 199).

From the early nineteenth century increasingly detailed records were kept of the incidence of disease, and efforts were made to account for its spread, including considering housing conditions. 'Among the inhabitants of the cellars and these back houses, the typhus is constantly present, and the number of persons under this disease that apply for medical assistance to the charitable institutions, the public will be astonished to hear, exceeds 3,000 annually' (Currie 1805, 203–4). Shimmin describes a family he met at Hodson Street as 'hard working and respectable', and raged about their child being sick with typhus, 'a young life endangered by the abominable but easily curable unhealthiness of the neighbourhood' (Shimmin 1883, 25–6).

It became evident that poor-quality housing was contributing to poor health in Liverpool: 'The vicious construction of the dwellings … the [inadequate] supply of privies and ash pits, and the state of the drainage and sewerage' (Duncan 1843, 12). The state of cleanliness of the courts was a cause for considerable concern in the 1850s and 1860s. In a report to the Board of Health in 1862, James Newlands reported that the corporation had taken up its powers under the Sanitation Act to enforce cleanliness, and had endeavoured to formalize the numbering of the houses within the courts and list their occupants in order that prosecutions could be sought if a court was not maintained. Hope frequently commented on the cleanliness or, more often, dirtiness of the courts he visited. For example, in a court he visited in 1883 where

A bathtub hangs outside a house in a court off Park Road in 1931
© Liverpool Record Office, Liverpool Libraries

A gully-flushing gang work to clean the drains in a Liverpool court
© Liverpool Record Office, Liverpool Libraries

he found four sick children, he noted that there were 'cellars containing vegetable remains' (Hope 1883–88, 21). Shimmin describes a similar scene: 'The street was sloppy, and strewed with decaying vegetables, and yet, amidst all, young children tried to gambol about' (1862, 130).

While history records little by way of intimate detail of personal hygiene and untidiness, there is evidence that many people living in even the most undesirable conditions maintained personal cleanliness. While some photographs show dirty courtyards, other present courtyards free of litter and with bathtubs hanging for storage outside tiny homes.

Before the connection of courts to a sewerage system, they had earth closets or middens where household waste and excreta were collected before being removed by night soil men.

> The duty of washing courts, passages, and places of deposit after the emptying of middens, was imposed on the nightmen under their contract, but it never was efficiently performed, owing chiefly to the condition in the contract, which made it imperative to wash only when a public hydrant was within thirty yards of the place. This restriction left more than half of the places unwashed. (Newlands 1863, 10)

The 'night soil' would have been taken out of the town and used as fertilizer on surrounding countryside. Evidence of this was found when small fragments of eighteenth-century pottery were discovered during archaeological excavations in Calderstones Park, an area known to have had prehistoric activity, but not occupied in the eighteenth century (Speakman et al. 2015, 36).

While criticism of 'lazy and negligent householders' living in court housing is found in contemporary commentary (*Liverpool Mercury*, 1 May 1900, 9), it was sometimes those in work who were blamed for undertaking dirty jobs in the courts: 'The flagging of courts and passages is laid and maintained by the owner or owners, but it often happens that the surface of a court gets out of order, particularly in courts occupied by oakum pickers and chip dealers, who use the flagged area as a workshop' (Newlands 1863, 28).

The spread of typhus was, in part, linked to the conditions of court housing. Hope recorded cases of people with communicable diseases, and some of the conditions they were living in:

> Typhus; about 6th or 7th day. Tunnel entrance to this filthy and abominable court house is so dark as to necessitate a lamp to examine the patient. The people are very poor – 6 in a room – almost bare of furniture; everything foul and filthy; people clothed with rags, children 3 parts naked + bearing evidence of chronic starvation. (Hope 1883–88, 124)

Overcrowding

Following a massive increase in population, overcrowding was considered to be a severe problem in Liverpool's courts by the mid-nineteenth century, and was quantified by contemporary observers. It was sometimes the density of the housing itself which was of concern; for example, in 1863 Newlands found 92 houses in six courts off Blenheim Street. In other cases it was the number of people living in each home that was shocking. In 1851 No. 1, Edwards Buildings on Clay Street was inhabited by 16 people: a couple and their three sons, a servant, and ten lodgers, all adults aged 18 to 37. Another court house off Clay Street in the same year recorded 13 inhabitants, including three women with babies: one married, living in this overcrowded house with her husband and daughter, one recorded as widowed, the other married, but with her husband not living there, possibly away at sea.

Journalists who visited the courts made particular reference to the number of people they found living in these homes: 'to see the women and children pouring out from every court, house and cellar, and many of them looking well and hearty was surprising: and wonder might be excited as to where all these found room to lie down' (Shimmin 1862, 110). The causes of the overcrowding, especially sub-letting, are also cause for comment: 'The room is perhaps eight or nine feet square. Into the boards is ground the dirt of years ... The circumstances suggested, although the woman below denied it, that the bedroom was sub-let to a separate family' (Shimmin 1883, 18).

The levels of overcrowding are clear today through statistical analysis undertaken on census data: '36.8% of (mostly smaller) back houses contained six or more people and 20.4% of occupied cellars had at least six inhabitants' (Pooley 2006, 209–10). The impact of this overcrowding was a contemporary concern, as it was seen to threaten the health of the inhabitants.

> When other circumstances are taken into account such as the dense population and abominably filthy state of many of the courts, it is easy to understand in what way the construction of these dwellings may contribute to swell the mortality of Liverpool. (Duncan 1843, 10)

A government inquiry into the condition of working-class housing in 1885 recorded interviews with local protagonists on the subject. The view of the City Engineer, Clement Dunscombe, was that around 70,000 people in the 'poorest' classes remained in overcrowded and unhealthy dwellings (Royal Commission on the Housing of the Working Classes 1885, 505). Anger was felt that people's lives and health were being put at risk: 'It is not that there are more courts in Liverpool than in other towns ... but so freely has human life been sacrificed here, rather than that land should be sacrificed' (Thom 1845).

With high mortality rates, death would have been a conspicuous element of life for people in Victorian cities. The presence of corpses in houses for some days after death was common practice while plans were being made for burial.

Visiting the corpse was part of the grieving ritual linked to faiths and cultures in Liverpool's courts, and wakes were also held in the home. The presence of a corpse in the house was a cause for concern as it could encourage the spread of some diseases (Strange 2005, 67–9). The Medical Officer of Health for Liverpool, Edward Hope, described a visit to a court where two teenage girls were suffering from typhus, while the dead body of their mother was lying in the house and had been there for two days (Hope 1883–88, 56).

'there are thousands of houses and hundreds of courts ... without a single drain of any description, and I never hail anything with greater delight than I do a violent tempest or a terrific thunderstorm accompanied by heavy rain, for these are the only scavengers that thousands have to cleanse away impurities and the filth in which they live or, rather, exist.'

George Buchanan (1831–95)

Analytical work exploring the reasons for the spread of disease developed from the mid-nineteenth century onwards. As theories of miasma were superseded, it was possible for scientists to look at other possible factors and assess their impact. In 1864 Dr George Buchanan published a detailed work in which he brought together data about the spread of 'fever', the common contemporary term for typhus.

Buchanan had followed his father into the medical profession, becoming physician at the London Fever Hospital from 1861. He increasingly worked in public health, undertaking research in Liverpool in the early 1860s, in which he explored the spread of typhus. Different types of typhus are caused by different rickettsia bacteria, spread variously by lice, fleas, mites or ticks. While lifestyle and living conditions could be linked to this, Buchanan was able to dispel some myths, notably demonstrating that the 'Irish pauper class' was not especially susceptible to 'epidemic fever' (primarily typhus) (Buchanan 1864, 9). He did not find a link between occupation and typhus. He did, however, find that housing, drainage and density of population were significant factors. Buchanan reported that personal factors influenced susceptibility, including uncleanliness, age and diet (1864, 441–2). He is nuanced in his consideration of the role alcohol played, accepting that the cost deprived people of meat, but describing missionary reports of 'no destitution except what is the result of drink' as biased (1864, 22).

Buchanan discusses the impacts of legislative control on building, referring to sewerage being constructed under the 1846 Sanitary Act, and housing construction improving following the Liverpool Building Act of 1842. He expressed concern that while new building conformed, 'no attempt was made to deal with the old standing conditions that made Liverpool so unhealthy a town'. Only the 1864 Sanitary Amendment Act, he suggested, could force owners of buildings or the corporation to improve buildings, or demolish them if necessary (1864, 24).

Throughout his career Buchanan's achievements were recognized: he was elected a fellow of the Royal College of Physicians of London in 1866 and fellow of the Royal Society in 1882. He was knighted in 1892.

'Most of the courts are well paved; many have stand pipes for the supply of water (and which at the time of our visit was always on); and galvanized iron [rubbish] receptacles'

8

Life in
the courts

While court housing was very common in Liverpool, the experience of life in the courts would have varied considerably over time, and in different areas. The building standard of the housing, the density of the population, and the maintenance of the buildings and services would have generated very different qualities of home for different people in different courts.

Contemporary descriptions were generally written and published for political reasons, largely campaigning for better housing, so they can be highly emotive:

> I visited many families of this description ... (breadwinner was unemployed) ... in houses, rooms and cellars; the children almost in a state of nudity, and it was impossible to look upon them without seeing hunger and starvation depicted in their countenances. Their habitations completely destitute of bedding, or any kind of furniture and sleeping on shavings or straw covered by a wrapper or a couple of sacks. (Finch 1842, 89)

The financial situation of many families would have been precarious. By the nineteenth century Liverpool's economy relied on the docks: 'Liverpool's social and occupational structure, as well as its local economy, was shaped by its transport, commercial and port activities' (Anderson 1983, 79). The nature of the dock work which employed thousands of people in Liverpool was deeply insecure, workers being hired by the half-day. Although 'some dockers were paid relatively high hourly wages, the number of hours they were able to work in a given week fluctuated alarmingly' (Milne 2006, 303). As Liverpool's economy in the nineteenth century grew to rely on casual labour, income insecurity would have resulted in phases of poverty, especially when the supply of labour outstripped demand, causing under- or unemployment.

The only nineteenth-century account of court housing attributed to someone who actually lived in a court describes a typical court of a standard layout. This un-named author refers to an example off Vauxhall Road, which would have been built around the 1840s, and was thus some forty years old at the time the description was published. It is described as having 'battered remains of what was once a flagged pavement', a cellar with a 'perennially damp floor' and a house with a 'narrow dilapidated stair' (*Liverpool Mercury*, 25 December 1882, 6).

The communal space of a court with washing equipment
© Liverpool Record Office, Liverpool Libraries

The casual nature of labour on the docks necessitated living nearby so as to be at hand when work was available. There was therefore high demand for housing near the docks, stimulating the building of high-density housing, mainly courts.

> If some maritime workers could, over time, live further afield, Liverpool's dockers always had to live near the waterfront, and the expansion of the dock system from the mid-nineteenth century meant that there could never be a single dockers' district. Dock work, no matter how skilled or specialized, was casual labour, with hiring stands operating in the morning and in the middle of the day. This dictated all its characteristics, and not least its geography. (Milne 2006, 303)

While there was an important movement to improve housing, many nineteenth-century accounts reveal opinions regarding why people lived in courts that are underlain by the judgmental, sometimes racist or sexist views of the onlookers. Several characteristics of life in court housing are explored repeatedly in nineteenth-century descriptions, including employment, crime, health, alcohol abuse, food supply and the role of religion.

> The husband is in constant employment, and was said to be very steady, but how he could reconcile himself to look daily upon the amicable union of filth and laziness which his house exhibited was a puzzle. The convenience of his home to his labour was given as the reason for remaining in such a doghole … The woman was sallow, but lively, and although her children had weak eyes and a sickly look, were streaked with dirt and gnawed at chunks of bread whilst staring at us, the mother said they never seemed to ail much. (Shimmin 1864, 11–12)

Crime

A popular association grew up between court housing and crime. The semi-private shared spaces of courtyards were often valuable communal spaces, but in some places they seemed to provide an ideal setting for criminal activity. Alleys were potential escape routes to those who knew them well.

Literary descriptions of events set in courts and alleys reinforced this perception. In *Sketches By Boz*, Dickens reflects the dirtiness of the alley houses with the crime there: 'The alley into which he turned, might, for filth and misery, have competed with the darkest corner of this ancient sanctuary in its dirtiest and most lawless time' (Dickens 1836, 358). In *A Child of the Jago*, the characters use the courts and alleys as escape routes: 'Dicky … carried his way deviously towards home. Working through the parts beyond Jago Row, he fetched round into Honey Lane … [and] … slipped through the passage, and so, by the back yard crawled through the broken fence into the court' (Morrison 1896, 36–7).

While nineteenth-century newspaper reports are full of references to incidents in Liverpool's courts, the addresses recorded for lawbreakers in general do not suggest a significant difference in levels of crime between courts and other types of housing. Using newspaper reports, it has been established that around one-fifth of the brothels located and reported on between 1851 and 1873 were in courts or cellars. About another fifth were in individually numbered street-front houses. The rest are located only by street, and so could have been in courts or street-front houses (Bennett 2018).

Overcrowding and poor living conditions have been linked to lawbreaking, but it could have been efforts to improve housing that drove criminal behaviour, with people made homeless by the clearance of cellars being forced into an underworld: breaking into vacant buildings to squat, and begging or stealing to survive (Macilwee 2011, 91).

Alcohol

Several contemporary writers identified alcohol as a contributory factor to the poor conditions in which people lived. Hugh Shimmin repeatedly revisits drink as a theme in his writing about Liverpool working-class life, reflecting his own experiences with an alcoholic father (Walton and Wilcox 1991, 4). The Revd Abraham Hume reviewed the religious and social condition of Liverpool in 1858, finding that 'Immorality assumes many forms, but two are usually prominent. These are "Intemperance" and what is called the "Social Evil" [prostitution]. The former is often the parent of the latter' (Hume 1858, 28). Hume's view was that it was not surprising that the poor turned for solace to drink, and he advocated a role for the Church in presenting alternatives.

The impact of alcoholism in driving poverty was a great concern: 'A copper ore worker, earning 27s a week, all of which is spent in drink by himself and his wife. The children are in rags and look idiotic. In the same street, there are sober men, earning only 20s and 23s a week, who are living in comfort' (Parkes and Sanderson 1871, 68).

Alcohol was recognized as a fuel to violence, and there was especial concern for children living with alcoholic parents. On 3 June 1875 the *Liverpool Mercury* reported the story of a 12-year-old girl, Mary Ann McKechnie, who was in prison for drunkenness, and whose mother had been found drunk the same day. She was released to her father. In other cases, children were recorded as having been accidentally smothered by parents sleeping with them while drunk (Walton and Wilcox 1991, 134–45). Hope wrote about the situation he found in court houses that he visited: 'child sitting half dressed at foot of staircase. Infected, face flushed, pink extra-vasation all over body. Crowd of women and children about. 3 roomed house. Filthy dirty. Mother in a disgustingly filthy state; fat, drunken, tremulous and sweating; strong odour' (Hope 1883–88, 32).

A social reaction against the damaging effects of alcohol spurred the temperance movement. The Liverpool Temperance Society was founded in 1830 (Macilwee 2011, 115). It was one of a number of temperance societies formed that year, including England's first in Bradford, followed by Warrington, Manchester, Bristol and London. In Liverpool other independent societies grew up in the following decades, some linked to existing organizations and churches. The Total Abstinence League of the Cross was founded in 1875, linked to the Catholic Church. Toxteth Park banned pubs in 1890, becoming the largest area of prohibition in England (Macilwee 2011, 115–16).

To meet the growing demand for non-alcoholic drinks, temperance bars and hotels were established and cocoa rooms sprang up.

Pamphlets published in Liverpool recited the ills of alcohol and advocated temperance: 'There are bright spots as well as dark spots on the Mersey. We need not go to Maine or to the States of America to witness the advantages of Prohibition' (Jones n.d.). The US state of Maine had passed a Prohibition Law in 1851, one of the first statutory controls in the American temperance movement. In the UK, the 'Direct Popular Veto' on alcohol was endorsed by the National Liberation Federation in 1889. The term 'black spot' was adopted by other temperance campaigners in Liverpool to refer to areas where alcohol use was rife (*Liverpool Mercury*, 30 November 1899).

Religion

The temperance movement was often promoted by religious groups, keen to get to the root of poor lifestyles and poor living conditions. The Liverpool Town Mission (later Liverpool City Mission) was formed in 1829 to provide moral and religious 'improvement' to the poor of Liverpool. Its early activities included 'agents' visiting homes, reading scripture and offering religious direction. Later, as more

A Liverpool court photographed in 1929,
showing a water standpipe
© Liverpool Record Office, Liverpool Libraries

funding was found from local merchants and business owners, mission halls were built in which people could gather, participate in religious activities, use libraries and enjoy the wholesome entertainment of games rooms (Read and Jebson 1979).

There was concern, however, that churches, mission halls and visiting missionary workers were not reaching out to people living in court housing. Shimmin proffered the view that priests never visited court houses, but bemoaned the fact that the Church collected tithes. He believed that visiting church could help people improve their living conditions, but despaired at the lack of churchgoing.

Despite these concerns, Shimmin credited the Revd Hume with social improvement in Everton: 'Dr Hume whose perseverance and energy are well known, and yet whose labours are not fully recognized, has been instrumental in ridding the neighbourhoods of a moral pestilence' (Shimmin 1862, 124).

While a lack of morality offended Shimmin, different faiths attracted criticism and intolerance from some quarters. In his last sermon before the closure of St Silas' Church, Pembroke Place, the Revd George E. Durham bemoaned the fact that the area's community was 'Catholics, Jews, heretics, those of queer faith and those of no faith' (*Daily Post*, 29 April 1940). Sectarian divisions between Catholics and Protestants were a distinctive element of Liverpool's nineteenth- and twentieth-century popular culture. While social conditions, religious beliefs and community relationships were complex, broad-brush criticism of 'the low Irish' was common, and court housing was popularly associated with those from Ireland or of Irish descent (Belchem and MacRaild 2006, 325–8). While new Irish refugee migrants, arriving in the wake of the Great Hunger, were most likely to live in courts, they were far from exclusive to the Irish, being the most common housing of working-class Liverpool.

Edward William Hope

Dr Edward William Hope was Assistant Medical Officer of Health for Liverpool from 1883 to 1894, and Medical Officer of Health from 1894 to 1924. Hope's initial appointment to the assistant role was as a result of an open letter from Dr Morrish to the incumbent Medical Officer of Health, Dr Stopford Taylor in 1883. The letter criticized Taylor in the context of a new outbreak of typhus, and highlighted the role of housing in this epidemic (Clayton n.d., 1; Morrish 1883).

Hope produced a unique historical resource, a set of notebooks about his experiences, which form a record of the social history of Liverpool. These books capture personal illness, and also record the conditions in which people were living and becoming ill. Hope comments on housing type, describing the cleanliness of people and their homes, the level of furnishing and the number of inhabitants. Hope also sometimes comments on employment, drunkness and individuals being in a state of starvation (Hope 1883–88).

Hope worked in a variety of public health fields, including infant and maternal health, communicative disease and hygiene. His detailed records and analysis captured the relevance of the housing situation of individuals, families and communities to public health concerns and increased mortality (Clayton n.d., 2–6).

'All extensions of the town should be made in accordance with a fixed plan, in combination with improvements in the direction and width of streets'

9

Housing legislation, control and change

Courts and alleys were developed as cheap housing for rental profit, but overcrowding and poor build quality meant many turned into 'slums'. Public health campaigners advocated greater legislation and control to improve conditions (Trench and Beard 1871, 10). Urban development was regulated from the post-medieval period. The earliest regulation of buildings relied on the goodwill of town residents: as towns started to grow rapidly in the sixteenth and seventeenth centuries, limits on pollution, the prevention of overcrowding and control of building and development began to be considered. In London this was formalized through the legal system, common law and royal proclamations (Barnes 1970). From the eighteenth century to the mid-nineteenth century Acts of Parliament were sought individually by town corporations rather than being made applicable across the whole of Britain. Liverpool Corporation applied for legislative control through the Liverpool Improvement Bill 1803, which demanded that no cellars should be built with an opening lower than 3 feet above street level, no court could be less than 18 feet wide, and each court had to have an open entrance (Ley 2000, 6; Taylor 1970, 85). However, this Bill never became an Act of Parliament. James Newlands said of it, 'the interest of different individuals being affected by the Bill, the old cry of rights of property was as usual raised in defence of the wrongs of poverty, and inferior considerations triumphed over public good' (Newlands 1858, 11).

There was an impetus to replace the older 'closed' courts with 'open courts'. These had a wide uncovered entrance from the street, and were more like narrow cul-de-sacs. In some cases the end of the court away from the road also opened on to an

Table 1 Nineteenth-century Acts of Parliament concerned with housing and public health

Date	Act of Parliament	Impact
1825	Liverpool Building Act	Increased required space between houses to prevent spread of fire; restrictions around chimneys; drains must be covered
1842	Liverpool Building Act	Local Act with sections on building, including building size and construction, fire prevention, and provision of services, including privies
1844	Metropolitan Building Act	Effectively banned back-to-back houses in London
1846	Liverpool Sanitary Act	Local Act to improve public health, bringing into existence roles of Medical Officer of Health, Borough Engineer and Inspector of Nuisances
1847	Towns Improvement Clauses	Houses to be built with drains
1848	Public Health Act	First national Act to deal with public health issues, not compulsory in municipal towns; established central Board of Health
1858	Local Government Act	Towns empowered to adopt clauses more easily from the Towns Improvement Clauses (see above) through bye-laws
1866	Public Health Act (Sanitary Act)	Local authorities compelled to remove 'nuisances' and provide sewerage (to be connected to all houses), water and street cleaning; limited use of cellars for living, and defined and controlled overcrowding; creation of Royal Sanitary Commission
1866	Dwelling Houses Act	First national legislation to allow local authority housing
1872	Public Health Act	Created Health Authority districts with public health officers
1875	Artisans Dwelling Act	Allowed local authorities to buy and demolish 'slum' areas
1875	Public Health Act	Bolstered 1866 Sanitary Act in requirements of local authorities to maintain cleanliness and provide services of sewerage, water, street cleaning; systematized reporting of contagious disease to local Medical Officers of Health
1885	Housing of the Working Classes Act	Landlords made more responsible to maintain houses they let in good condition
1889	Liverpool Act	Courts must be open at both ends, 30 feet wide and a maximum of 100 feet long
1890	Public Health (Amendment) Act	Consolidation of previous Acts to strengthen powers through bye-laws

alley, which meant there was more space and light. The houses of open courts were not always back-to-back, some having access to the rear via an alley, although a study of all Liverpool courts in 1863 found that 93% of them were back-to-back (Newlands 1863, 28–9).

In some parts of Liverpool, restrictions on building were imposed through land transfers, which prevented the development of court housing. For example, a transfer of ownership record from 1831 for a piece of land off Canning Street states that the area must not be used 'to carry on offensive trades nor erect any courts or backhouses or any steam engine houses to be built according to the elevation approved not to build to exceed 60 feet in height. To keep areas in good repair not to put out workhouse doors' (LVRO Deeds and Surrendered Titles 352 CLE CON 5/21).

Reports of the standard of living in courts helped to forge opinion in favour of action and legislation to improve the standard of housing. While there was some control on new building, Newlands accepted, in 1848, that court housing was not going to be cleared away imminently, and instead suggested some elements of shared facilities:

'by having a common kitchen, washing, and baking establishment. Such courts as these would be convenient, healthy and economical' (Newlands 1848, 109).

The Liverpool Building Act 1825

The first Liverpool Building Act was concerned with the density of building in terms of the spread of fire. Narrow access from the street, narrow courtyards and small houses would have provided limited space for inhabitants, and would have exacerbated the spread of fire. The Liverpool Building Act of 1825 focused on this threat. It also prohibited the discharge of smoke from the front of buildings. From plans drawn up by city engineers and archive photographs it is clear that many court houses had fireplaces built in, but this law implies that temporary braziers may have been in use in some rooms of court or cellar dwellings. This would have caused pollution within the ill-ventilated courtyards. The Act also required water from buildings to be conveyed into drains.

Public health officials and campaigners continued to keep up the pressure for reform, and utilized ongoing research extensively in this. Chadwick's *Sanitary Condition* report identified high mortality rates in many of Britain's industrial towns. Chadwick argued that the cost of providing sewers, water supplies and paving would be lower than the amount spent on treating people who became ill as a direct result of living in poor conditions (Chadwick 1842, 188–211). Chadwick's proposed solutions centred around rebuilding and more formal town planning, rather than Building Acts that were applied individually, which he found to be inconsistently enforced and often evaded (Chadwick 1842, 287). Developing on this approach, a few years later James Newlands stated that

> All extensions of the town should be made in accordance with a fixed plan, in combination with improvements in the direction and width of streets ... It is only by a plan so comprehensive that errors introduced by want of foresight can be remedied, and evils caused by sordid covetousness can be palliated or eradicated. (Newlands 1848, 104–5)

Liverpool responded to this research and campaigning, and improved its 1825 Building Act in 1842. This was again interested in fire protection, and required the use of non-combustible materials or large timbers for floors and roofs,

and increased chimney heights. To improve living conditions there were also requirements for better ventilation, and set room heights and window sizes for habitable rooms, restrictions on the use of cellars, and the empowerment of local magistrates to order the cleansing, at the owners' expense, of any 'filthy or unwholesome house' (Ley 2000, 12–19; Farrer and Brownbill 1966, 39).

Health of Towns

In 1841 the Health of Towns Select Committee looked into housing, among other issues regarding the health of people living in urban areas. They identified the fact that although some towns had instituted Building Acts, these were not universal, and were non-standard in their remit. As a result of the Select Committee's report, a group of three Bills was proposed in 1841 by the Home Secretary, the Marquis of Normanby: the Buildings Regulation Bill, the Boroughs Improvement Bill and the Drainage of Towns Bill.

Debate around the Boroughs Improvement Bill in 1841 faced appeals for the exclusion of some urban areas, and it was combined with the Buildings Regulation Bill in 1842. This aimed to appoint town surveyors for all towns, outlaw the building of back-to-back housing, effectively prevent cellar dwelling, make all court housing open to the street and of a maximum length, set standards for the width of streets and courts and make the provision of privies compulsory (Ley 2000, 12–19; Farrer and Brownbill 1966, 39). However, the Bill was opposed by the Duke of Buccleuch, who argued that cellar dwelling in Liverpool provided homes, and that the effects of the Bill would be negative:

> As to the miserable condition of dwellings in cellars, to which the noble Lord alluded, he would refer him to the town of Liverpool, with respect to which an Act had been passed which touched on the subject. It appeared that 22,000 of the poorer classes of that place resided in cellars, from which they would be ejected on the 1st of July, if the Local Act to which he had just alluded was carried into effect. (Hansard, 11 June 1844, vol. 75, cc. 479–84)

The argument that rents would increase provoked concern that this would force more people to live in temporary lodgings rather than have more permanent rented homes. It was feared that in the long term this could lead to large numbers of untenanted houses, and rapid decline in the repair of buildings and ultimately the social cohesion of some areas. Although

better housing seemed socially desirable, it was argued that it was an economic impossibility at that time (Burnett 1978, 76). This led to Liverpool's being granted an exemption from the Act. Eventually the Bill failed to be passed into law.

The Drainage of Towns Bill was debated in the House of Lords between January and May 1841. Lord Ellenborough commended the Marquess of Normanby for bringing it to the house, saying he had 'read the evidence with the greatest pain and apprehension, and with greatest compassion for those who were compelled to inhabit the dwellings referred to' (Hansard, 29 January 1841, vol. 56, cc. 138–9). However, the Bill lost momentum, and it was concluded that change would require taxation, which was outside the remit of the House of Lords.

Following the failure of the Buildings Regulation Bill, the Health of Towns Commission was appointed on 9 May 1843. The Duke of Buccleuch was chairman of the Commission, which looked at 50 towns with high mortality rates, covering a population of over three million people. It reviewed street conditions such as paving and cleaning, drainage and water supply, and the construction and ventilation of new buildings. Evidence was taken from a number of individuals. A builder from Liverpool, Samuel Holmes, explained that the courts and alleys which are inaccessible to carts are not cleansed by the parochial authorities, but are left to the inhabitants to cleanse or not at their pleasure; and the result is that a great number of courts inhabited by the lower orders receive little or no cleansing except that which Providence showers from the clouds. (Commissioners for Inquiring into the State of Large Towns and Populous Districts 1844, 275)

The commission concluded that building regulation was unnecessary and would interfere with structural stability and fire regulation. It did recommend minimum widths for courts and alleys, that the heights of buildings should be proportional to the size of the court – to increase light and ventilation – and that the habitation of cellars should only be allowed where they had proper foundations, drainage, large fireplaces and open spaces in front of them. It also recommended that better surveyors be appointed under local Improvement Acts. This reiterated much of what had been put forward by Chadwick in 1842, and discussed in the Buildings Regulation Bill (Martin

Gaskell, 1983). The commission's work resulted in the Health of Towns Bill 1845 which dealt with sewerage, drainage and water supply. Because of concerns over the perception of interference, the Bill did not include detail on building control.

When the Health of Towns Bill was again debated in the House of Commons in 1847–48, it was introduced by Viscount Morpeth, who said, 'It must be admitted that, on the whole, the Health of Towns Bill is an excellent measure … it seeks to secure water, pure air, and a little sunshine for the inhabitants of cities – now so large, active, and important a part of the population' (Hansard, 18 June 1847, vol. 93, cc. 727–53). Through the months in which it was debated and amended, consideration was given as to whether or not London should be included in the Bill, whether laws should be applied only prospectively or retrospectively as well, and where the money should come from for improvements – Liverpool being cited as an example of a town able to afford its own improvements (Lord John Russell, Hansard, 5 July 1847, vol. 93, cc. 1186–92).

The debate on the Health of

Towns Bill was heated. One speaker, Mr Hudson, MP for Sunderland, opposed the Bill. He suggested that local corporations should be enabled to make provision for sanitary improvements and housing regulations for themselves: 'The people wanted to be left to manage their own affairs; they did not want Parliament to be so paternal as it wished to be – interfering in everybody's business, and, like all who so interfered, not doing its own well' (Hansard, 18 June 1847, vol. 93, cc. 727–53). In opposition to this view, Mr Wakelye read a letter from Dr Laycock:

> Mr. Hudson has no knowledge of the sanitary condition of the city; he probably never visited a poor sick person in his life … For several years past I have visited the sick poor of York gratuitously, and without any regard to personal inconvenience. This has continually brought me into the courts and alleys of the city, and the impression left on my mind is quite opposed to that which Mr. Hudson has expressed. (Hansard, 18 June 1847, vol. 93, cc. 727–53)

Hudson retorted that 'during the period of the cholera, when others were deterred by the fear of contagion, he devoted a considerable portion of his time to the purpose of visiting and relieving those who were afflicted'

(Hansard, 18 June 1847, vol. 93, cc. 727–53).

The Bill was adopted as the Public Health Act 1848, which worked in parallel with the Nuisance Removal and Diseases Prevention Act, which operated in areas where the Public Health Act was not in force. London operated under the Metropolitan Commission of Sewers Act. The Acts created a General Board of Health, which continued to report annually until 1858 (Glen 1952, 3). They enforced proper provision for water supplies and drainage, supported through local taxes to fund improvements. The Acts met with broad approval, as they made provision for such significant improvements as all new houses having a toilet or ashpit. Many, however, felt that the legislation could have gone further.

Almost immediately after it was established, the General Board of Health had to face a large-scale cholera outbreak, which struck London, Edinburgh, Glasgow, Dundee, Manchester, Bristol, Liverpool, Hull and other major towns in 1848–49 (General Board of Health 1850, 16–17). It was felt in many towns that the lack of legislation relating to the density of building was a causal factor in the epidemic:

> LIVERPOOL – The preventative measures were carried out in this large town under the superintendence of Dr Duncan,

officer of health to the borough, who states that the chief localizing causes of the epidemic were 'The ordinary local and removable causes of disease; to wit, filth, want of drainage, offensive cesspools &c., and particularly overcrowding', over last of which, however, the authorities have no power. (General Board of Health 1850, Appendix A 111)

In 1867, following the next cholera outbreak, the Medical Officer of Health recommended the 'total demolition' of 387 houses to counteract typhus and cholera epidemics (Trench 1868, 30).

The Liverpool Building Act 1842

While progress was sporadic nationally, specific action was also taken locally. The Liverpool Building Act of 1842 described some of the conditions in relation to health: '[courts] are unfit for human habitation, and fevers and other diseases are constantly generated there'. The Act underlined that it was 'expedient that provision for the remedy thereof, and also that further provision be made for the regulation of future courts and alleys'. This Act demanded that every street be a minimum of 24 feet wide, and every court a minimum of 15 feet wide. The use of cellars

as dwellings was forbidden, though it continued for many decades. However, the Act was not able to enforce sufficient change to bring dwellings up to a good standard. Two decades later the Medical Officer of Health was still using the same phrasing when describing housing: 'the courts and alleys, which houses, by reasons of defects in the construction thereof, or the want of ventilation or proper conveniences, or from other causes, are unfit for human habitation' (Trench 1865, 1).

Building and sanitary controls

When the Public Health Act 1848 and the Nuisance Removal and Diseases Prevention Act 1846 were enacted they still faced considerable opposition. The Public Health Act was applied to 170 towns where local health boards were in place by 1854. There was varied opinion about the role, impact and effectiveness of the Act in different areas. It was used as a test case in arguments around the centralization of law, as opposed to legal autonomy for individual towns. Edwin Chadwick was attacked by Joshua Toulmin Smith and others for his 'anti-centralist' approach of delegating responsibility to individual local authorities (Claeys 1989, 317).

In Liverpool there are suggestions that activities to try to improve the sanitary conditions of courts met with differing responses from owners and residents:

> The materials for lime-washing the courts were provided by the Boards of Health, the actual work being carried out by gangs of paupers provided by the Parish Authorities. Lime-washing the exterior of the courts was unpalatable to many of the owners, who objected to it on the grounds that it would deteriorate the value of their property; the occupiers, however, took a different view of the case. (Hope 1931, 49)

In the mid-nineteenth century there was a change in emphasis from national legislation on public health and housing towards local control. The Local Government Act of 1858 enabled local governments to administer more public health initiatives and controls in their localities (Ley 2000, 42). It was through a local bye-law that Liverpool made back-to-back building illegal, via the Sanitary Amendment Act in 1864 (Burnett 1978, 155). This type of housing continued to be built in some towns as no bye-laws on open space around houses were obtained. Back-to-backs were still

built in Leeds, for example, up to 1936 (Ley 2000, 46).

Liverpool's 1864 Sanitary Amendment Act formed the basis of most housing improvement over the subsequent forty years. It placed controls on the nature of court developments, and provided the corporation with powers to purchase and demolish insanitary housing (Tarn 1969, 321). This 1864 Act was often used in conjunction with parallel national legislation such as the Housing Acts of 1866, 1875 and 1890 (Pooley 2006, 212). It was used to remove some courts, including those near slaughterhouses. In 1865 the corporation went further in controlling the amount of space around buildings, issuing a bye-law requiring all new houses to have a back yard of at least 150 square feet (Tarn 1969, 321). Following the outbreak of cholera in 1866, the 1865 Sewage Utilisation Act was amended to the Sanitary Act of 1866. This provided for drainage to houses, but did not extend far into building regulation.

As the worst types of house built by speculative developers were starting to be controlled, Liverpool Corporation was also beginning to utilize local legislation to build the first social housing in Britain.

St Martin's Cottages, opened in 1869, were built following the 1866 Dwelling Houses Act, which was the first national legislation to enable local authorities to construct housing and provide it to people as a means of social improvement. St Martin's Cottages, council housing constructed in tenement blocks, was completed in 1869. This municipal housing movement ran in parallel with the philanthropic development of housing by major employers, as seen at New Lanark in Scotland as early as the 1780s, Saltaire in West Yorkshire (1851), and later at Port Sunlight on Wirral and Bournville in Birmingham, both built at the turn of the nineteenth/twentieth centuries. Provision of housing in the mid-nineteenth century by charitable trusts such as the Peabody Foundation also transformed the quality of housing for many.

With attention from journalists and public health officials, public opinion started to support changes, including building regulations intended to improve living conditions. In 1868 the Royal Sanitary Commission was reappointed to enquire into the legal controls in place on sewerage, drainage, water supply, building control and administration and enforcement of these laws (Ley 2000, 59). The commission found that between 1848 and 1870 there was a multiplicity of Acts relating to aspects of public health and housing, and recognized that they were administered by numerous district councils for different geographical areas (Royal Sanitary Commission 1871, 4–14). The balance between local and national control for public health and housing was carefully described in its report. The commission concluded that for the benefit of public health and for economic reasons, effective sanitary legislation was required in a variety of areas including the supply of water and provision of sewerage, control of building, inspection of food, and registration of death and provision for burial (Ley 2000, 60). The first step towards universal provision of these necessities was the Local Government Board Act of 1871, which centralized the enforcement of public health laws. This challenged the anti-centralist political movement as it looked to apply living standards across all urban areas in England.

Bye-law housing

With new central controls, the Public Health Act of 1875 consolidated previous legislation and made it applicable country-wide. Mandatory requirements of the Act included adequate drainage to buildings, a sewer within 100 feet and fire-prevention features. The Act did not, however, represent a major step forward because areas of considerable concern which had not previously been addressed, such as damp, were still not legislated on (Ley 2000, 68). The requirements of the Public Health Act were significant enough to drive the development of terraced housing, which became known as 'bye-law housing', reflecting its compliance to the legal requirements. Alongside legislative changes, economic shifts saw incomes increase and the cost of food decrease, especially imported food from the Americas. This created conditions for a new style of better-quality housing: terraced houses with back yards were built across cities in Britain.

The pressure for ongoing improvement in housing conditions continued: 'Open out the blind courts, slowly and steadily demolish the blind houses, the existence of which is absolutely incompatible with good health, ruthlessly sweep away the few courts which are incapable of improvement and which are fatal nuclei of fever, and the death rate will soon decrease' (Shimmin 1883, 9). When improvements were made to housing, this too attracted attention, praise and relief at the improved conditions:

> the work of the Corporation is seen at once. Most of the courts are well paved; many have stand pipes for the supply of water (and which at the time of our visit was always on);

and galvanized iron receptacles, in which all the dry rubbish of the house is put, are placed in convenient situations. Almost every court is well drained. (Parkes and Sanderson 1871, 69)

It was asserted that failure to improve conditions had directly contributed to deaths: 'it is no exaggeration to say that hundreds of lives have been cynically sacrificed' (Shimmin 1883, 8).

Further controls were introduced on the subdivision of buildings: 'the use of cellars or underground rooms as separate dwellings is under strict regulations' (Duff 1884, 26). Some cellars were filled in with rubbish, but became dangers in themselves to the residents of the courts, especially children. Cellars continued to be a rubbish trap in the twentieth century: 'There were loads of houses ... with cellars full of rubbish' (Angela Rooney, on living in court housing in Johnson Terrace in the 1940s and 1950s, Museum of Liverpool oral history collection). Some cellars continued in use:

> Kenny's mother, my Auntie Lucy, used to do her washing in our cellar because ... They had no washing facilities in the court house. In Jane's parents' house where they moved to they had in the cellar was like cobbles, street cobbles and in the corner was a ... a wringing machine ... boiler.

No it wasn't, it was like a big copper that you had to light a fire underneath and that would heat the water. They used to boil the Christmas puddings in it. (Jean Tyrell and Kenneth Smith, on living in a court in Mann Street in the 1940s and 1950s, Museum of Liverpool oral history collection)

In 1889 the Liverpool Act effectively made it uneconomic to attempt to build any form of court housing. Controls required newly built courts to be open to the highway at both ends, to be 30 feet wide and no longer than 100 feet long. They could have no more than 23 houses in them (Tarn 1969, 322). This made it impossible to construct the worst types of housing. 'There appears to be no reason to doubt that under the proper conditions private enterprise could do its part in providing for the deficiency in houses, demolishing insanitary property and rebuilding where possible on the cleared areas' (Liverpool Corporation 1918). This type of legislation in Liverpool and around the country led to a focus on the construction of terraced housing.

Acts of Parliament were applicable to new buildings, and older court buildings were not required to be altered, but problems such as a lack of light and air moving around the courts had been identified. Wholesale demolition and rebuilding of some areas was not always possible, so other approaches were suggested, including the insertion of 'through houses' or gaps in the layout of the courts, a solution that was occasionally employed (Burnett 1978, 74).

Slum clearance and rehousing

Court housing gained a reputation as 'slum' housing, and active work was undertaken to move people into better homes. However, not all people living in courts in the mid-twentieth century remember them as slums. A series of memories captured as oral histories in the Museum of Liverpool collection describe a different view:

> well [courts being considered slum housing] ... is totally unfounded, people found themselves ... were born into those conditions, there were some lovely people, you know ... All history is contemporary history, they say, it can only be understood in its own time, the values – their morals and their values and everything else about it. (Bernard Rowan, on living in a court off Saltney Street in the 1940s and 1950s, Museum of Liverpool oral history collection)

As courts aged, their pre-existing variation in build quality was only exacerbated. 'The houses are small, old and in many cases dilapidated' (Shimmin 1862, 123).

Some courts deteriorated over time: 'The dismal courts, and wretched crumbling streets, some of which by the way – Sawney Pope Street, for example – contained, many years ago rather fashionable residences, are now inhabited by a hand-to-mouth living population of the most extraordinary description' (Shimmin 1883, 9–10). Meanwhile other courts continued to be home to professional people; it may have been that these were not targeted for demolition and so stood for longer. For example, Watkinson's Buildings and Watkinson's Terrace, the last surviving example of court housing off Pembroke Place, were homes in the 1860s–1890s to people in a range of jobs, including police, fire police, upholstery, dock and railyway porters, tailors, customs officers, butchers and clerks.

The 1875 Artisans' Dwellings Act enabled local authorities to pull down and rebuild 'slum' areas. Clearance of the cellars led to a decline in mortality rates, but crowded the courts with more people seeking cheap housing there. The Health Committee of the town officially had control over the quality of court housing from the late nineteenth century, but in reality their powers were limited. Journalists such as Shimmin were not convinced of their effectiveness, complaining that they were obsessed with statistics (Walton and Wilcox 1991, 186).

Having provided early examples of social housing from the 1860s, Liverpool remained highly committed to it. Even after legislation in 1919 obliged all local authorities to make such provision, Liverpool continued to exceed the requirements (Pooley 2006, 209). This enabled the clearance of poorer-quality housing, a process that became a feature of Liverpool's cityscape in the early twentieth century. A former resident of court housing remembers seeing them demolished:

> In Canty – Canterbury Street – they had a crane like that with a chain on with a big solid ball on; I used to go on the sites and watch them like that for hours. They'd go like that and the ball would hit the side, that's how the knocked the buildings down, I used to love watching them – I was mezmerized. (Angela Rooney, Museum of Liverpool oral history collection)

In 1890 the Housing of the Working Classes Act granted town corporations powers to close insanitary dwellings, and from this time parts of Liverpool were earmarked as 'insanitary areas' and mapped in advance of rebuilding work. The corporation received reports about the classification of areas as insanitary, and quantification of the progress made towards demolition. For example, in 1903 450 tenements were built in the Hornby Street area, housing 2,446 people. Liverpool was highly effective in this regard, and the corporation managed 2,895 dwellings under local housing schemes by 1919 (Pooley 2006, 214). Courts and back-to-back housing were a particular target for redevelopment:

> The courts and alleys continue to decrease in number, owing to the demolition of low class property for the extension of business premises, or the removal of insanitary property by the Insanitary Property and Artizans Dwelling Committee. The number of courts and alleys scheduled for inspection in 1890 was 2,165, in 1895 it had fallen to 1,660. (Hope 1900, 65)

The programme of demolition continued until the 1970s, and annual reports of the Housing Committee on progress are logged in the Liverpool Corporation records. Reports quantify the housing that was deemed sub-standard, and the number of houses demolished and people moved; for example, in 1956: 'The demolition of only 347 dwellings has permitted the erection of 2,829 dwellings up to the present time and it is anticipated that an ultimate total of 3,500 dwellings could be erected if all the remaining sites were made available for housing purposes' (Semple 1956, 136). These reports also set out the plans and predictions for the progress of 'slum clearance' over several years: 'In this City there exist 80,000 sub-standard houses of which 26,000 must be demolished; 5,000 of these are for immediate action and the remainder in 5 or 10 years time' (Semple 1956, 136–7).

As 'slum' houses were cleared, in some areas they were replaced, and the corporation invested public funds in the improvement of housing through the late nineteenth and twentieth century. The Bevington Street dwellings was one of the first publicly funded housing projects where the homes were rented out directly from the corporation to the tenants. There was a drive to improve overall housing quality, but analysis of the rehousing process has questioned whether tenants had equal opportunities to obtain new housing (Pooley 1985).

In 1930 national legislation followed what was already taking place in Liverpool and some other urban areas, and the Slum Clearance Act encouraged the demolition of areas defined as 'slum housing'. However, the job was so large that progress sometimes seemed slow: 'In spite of an accelerating slum clearance programme, obsolete dwellings still remain a formidable problem in the city' (Alker 1963, 12). In 1965

Liverpool still had 92,000 unfit dwellings (Burnett 1978, 279). Some of the problem centred around the provision of new housing for people to move into before they could move out of homes that had been deemed 'unfit'. The Liverpool MP Bessie Braddock described the problem in her autobiography:

> So much of the Liverpool slums have gone that the remainder stand out all the more clearly … Their fabric is finished. Knock down one of a row, and the rest will fall down. I've seen this happen. Why are they still inhabited? Because there's nowhere to put the tenants. (Braddock and Braddock 1963, 118)

Official reports echoed this view: 'To a large extent, the progress of slum clearance is closely related to the availability of other houses for the inhabitants of the cleared dwellings, and therefore to the rate of house-building' (Alker 1963, 15). Alker looked holistically at house-building, employment and amenities in new or growing areas, including Skelmersdale, Ellesmere Port, Halewood and Cantril Farm. By the mid-twentieth century there was a pattern of out-migration from Liverpool to these areas of Merseyside, as well as to London and the south-east (Lawton and Pooley 1976).

The programmes of 'slum clearance' were so thorough in Liverpool that there is now very minimal physical evidence for court housing in the city. However, the lives lived in courts can be explored from a range of evidence.

Bessie Braddock (1899–1970)

Bessie Braddock, MP for Liverpool Exchange ward from 1945 to 1970, served during a period of large-scale redevelopment, 'slum clearance' and rehousing of people in Liverpool. She campaigned for better housing, frequently speaking in the House of Commons about housing in Liverpool and the desperate need for investment in new housing. She was sometimes frustrated by wide-ranging housing policy:

> I am a member of the Liverpool City Council and represent a constituency which has some of the worst slums in the country. Many people in Liverpool have been waiting a long time for housing accommodation, but they are now being made to wait even longer because of the Ministry's insistence that derequisitioning should take place on a certain date. (Hansard, 4 February 1960, vol. 616, c. 1262)

Braddock underlined the circumstances in Liverpool, comparing it to other major industrial cities, including Glasgow, and arguing for investment in housing:

> when it comes to slum clearance in Liverpool, the number of houses which need major repairs and amenities or which should be demolished because they are no use for housing purposes is over 88,000. An extra effort should be made to deal with problems of this sort. Although the housing department in Liverpool is doing all that it can in face of financial difficulty, something more needs to be done. I hope that the Minister will take special notice not only of Liverpool but of other areas with similar difficulties to see whether it is necessary to introduce special legislation to the effect that the building of luxury buildings will be restricted until people have decent accommodation in which to live. (Hansard, 2 May 1962, vol. 658, c. 1128)

Braddock's focus on housing and the urban environment was a factor in the sustained efforts to move people to better housing. This required the demolition of the 'slums' that court houses were considered to be. New housing was larger, better built and with better services. While there remains inequality in housing, and important ongoing campaigns for improvements, the 'slum clearance' work of the early-to-mid-twentieth century provided a better quality of life for thousands of people in Liverpool every year.

'So much of the Liverpool slums have gone that the remainder stand out all the more clearly … Their fabric is finished. Knock down one of a row, and the rest will fall down. I've seen this happen. Why are they still inhabited? Because there's nowhere to put the tenants.'

'the court appears
bright with the daylight;
and down it are seen
rough-headed urchins
running with their feet
bare, and bonnetless girls'

Conclusion

Court housing formed a very significant element of the experience of living in Liverpool from the late eighteenth to the early twentieth centuries. Already by the time of the first census in 1801 more than one in ten of Liverpool's population were living in courts, then known as 'back houses' (Pooley 2006, 176).

Extensive construction of court housing through the nineteenth century resulted from the rapid growth of the town of Liverpool as the port expanded. The in-migration of tens of thousands of new residents in the second half of the century contributed to massive population increase and demand for more housing. Court housing was quick to construct and provided small, cheap units to let. It was the small size of court homes that attracted some of the earliest criticism of them:

> The greatest fault that is to be observed in the houses of this town ... is the lowness of the rooms ... This error may, perhaps,

be attributed to the builders, who erect most of the new houses on their own accounts, upon speculation, and for sale, and who have no other view than such as are strictly economic and directly profitable. (Moss 1784, 57)

Court housing accentuated the enormous discrepancy between the lives of the wealthiest and the poorest in Liverpool. It was a physical manifestation of the social differences in Liverpool from the eighteenth to the twentieth centuries. This was underlined by Duncan, who wrote,

> Does any one suppose that if the inhabitants of Rodney Street and Abercromby Square were to exchange places with those of Vauxhall or Exchange Wards, leaving their spacious mansions to be occupied by the inhabitants of the latter district, while they took up residence in the filthy and miserable courts and cellars, of Vauxhall

or Exchange, – their relative command of the necessaries of life remaining undisturbed – does any one suppose that the relative mortality of the two classes would likewise remain unaltered? (Duncan 1843, 62)

As the often poorly built courts aged, some of Liverpool's housing came to exemplify the worst 'slums' in the country. Living conditions in some places in the town in the nineteenth and early twentieth centuries were such that both philanthropic and local and national government efforts were necessary to create more suitable accommodation for people, in response to the descriptions being published (O'Mara 1994). Having experienced the widest discrepancies between living conditions in the nineteenth century, Liverpool is now recognized as a pioneer in the provision of social housing.

Much of our knowledge about life in Liverpool's courts comes from photographic and descriptive contemporary records. 'Slum clearance' programmes in the early twentieth century were highly effective. As a result there are only limited extant remains of back-to-back and court housing in Liverpool. A fragmentary part of two courts survives on Pembroke Place, re-purposed as the back rooms of two shops. Other back-to-backs survive at Duke's Terrace off Duke

Street. These have been creatively renovated for modern use, their size increased by piercing the central spine dividing wall, and blanking some of the front doors. It is only through such extensive alteration that this once common type of house would now meet the standards expected for a modern home.

While the physical remains of Liverpool's court housing are rare and special survivors, there is strong historical evidence for their form and construction, and for the lives that were lived in them. This form of housing was a huge element of Liverpool's social history in the eighteenth and nineteenth centuries and survived into the twentieth. Maps, images and descriptions remain, though there are no nineteenth-century accounts of Liverpool court housing by named individuals who lived in them. Public health officers and journalists visited and wrote about them, but as one journalist admitted: 'we were glad to escape from the heated atmosphere and gabble of the vaults, and were well prepared to enjoy the calmness of home' (Shimmin 1864, 39).

As courts were demolished, new housing replaced them, built in lower densities for better quality of life. From historic maps, for example, it can be ascertained that an area of around 1 sq km off Burlington Street near Scotland Road in north Liverpool was once

Duke's Terrace back-to-back housing off Duke Street, converted to modern homes
© Trustees of National Museums Liverpool

occupied by over 50 court houses, together with 16 street-front properties (residential and commercial). This area is now occupied by nine modern houses and gardens.

Housing changes and develops over time, with new innovations, improving legislation and differing requirements from residents. Courts represent a phase of Liverpool's history, a period when the town grew very rapidly and more and more people needed homes every year. This was an era when people needed to live near their work as transport was limited; a period before the widespread development of modern sanitation and standards of cleanliness; a period of severe social deprivation for some; and a time when the differences between the richest and the poorest were at their most extreme.

Bibliography

Abbreviations

LMI Liverpool Medical Institution
LVRO Liverpool Record Office,
    Liverpool Libraries
RC Royal Collection
ULSC University of Liverpool Special
    Collections

Adshead, S. D. (1910). 'City
    Overcrowded; Tenements Poor'. *New
    York Times*, 26 August.
Alcock, N. (2005). 'Housing the Urban
    Poor in 1800: Courts in Atherstone and
    Coventry, Warwickshire'. *Vernacular
    Architecture*, 36, pp. 49–60.
Alker, T. (1963). *Ten Year Housing
    Programme*. City of Liverpool. LVRO H
    643 HOU.
Anderson, B. L. (1983). 'The Service
    Occupations of Nineteenth-Century
    Liverpool'. In B. L. Anderson and
    P. J. M. Stoney, *Commerce, Industry and
    Transport: Studies in Economic Change
    on Merseyside*. Liverpool: Liverpool
    University Press, pp. 77–94.
Barley, M. W. (1963). *The House and Home*.
    London: Vista Books.
Barnes, T. G. (1970). 'The Prerogative
    and Environmental Control of London
    Building in the Early Seventeenth
    Century: The Lost Opportunity'.
    California Law Review, 58.6, pp. 1332–63.
    http://www.jstor.org/stable/3479701
    (accessed 28 March 2019).
Beames, T. (1852). *The Rookeries of
    London*. London: Thomas Bosworth.

Beastall, J. (2017). Unpublished report
    on Census research on Pembroke
    Place. Galkoff's and Secret Life of
    Pembroke Place Project, Museum of
    Liverpool.
Belchem, J. (2000). *Merseypride: Essays
    in Liverpool Exceptionalism*. Liverpool:
    Liverpool University Press.
Belchem, J. (2007). *Irish, Catholic and
    Scouse: The History of the Liverpool
    Irish, 1800–1939*. Liverpool: Liverpool
    University Press.
Belchem, J., and MacRaild, D. M. (2006).
    'Cosmopolitan Liverpool'. In
    J. Belchem (ed.), *Liverpool 800: Culture,
    Character and History*. Liverpool:
    Liverpool University Press, pp. 311–91.
Bennett, S. (2018). Unpublished research
    on Liverpool brothels. Galkoff's and
    Secret Life of Pembroke Place project,
    Museum of Liverpool.
Booth, C. (1898/99). *Notebooks*. LSE
    BOOTH/B/350. https://booth.lse.ac.uk/
    notebooks/ (accessed 28 March 2019).
Braddock, J., and Braddock, B. (1963).
    The Braddocks. London: Macdonald.
British Medical Journal (1865). 'Special
    Correspondence: Liverpool'. *British
    Medical Journal*, 1.226, pp. 441–2.
Buchanan, G. (1864). *Report Upon
    Epidemic Fever in Liverpool*. LMI
    Pamphlet 320. London: Eyre and
    Spottiswoode.
Burnett, J. (1978). *A Social History of
    Housing 1815–1985*. London: Routledge.
Burrell, S., and Gill, G. (2005). 'The
    Liverpool Cholera Epidemic of 1832

and Anatomical Dissection – Medical Mistrust and Civil Unrest'. *Journal of the History of Medicine and Allied Sciences*, 60.4, pp. 478–98.

Caradog-Jones, D. (1934). *The Social Survey of Merseyside*. Liverpool: Liverpool University Press.

Carpenter, M. W. (2010). *Health, Medicine, and Society in Victorian England*. Santa Barbara, CA: ABC Clio.

Chadwick, E. (1842). *Report on an Inquiry into the Sanitary Condition of the Labouring Population of Great Britain*. London: HMSO.

Chalklin, C. W. (1974). *The Provincial Towns of Georgian England*. London: Edward Arnold.

Claeys, G. (1989). *Citizens and Saints: Politics and Anti-politics in Early British Socialism*. Cambridge: Cambridge University Press.

Clayton, J. (n.d.). 'Dr Edward William Hope, Medical Officer of Health for Liverpool 1894–1924: Development of an International Public Health Authority'. http://www.evolve360. co.uk/Data/10/Docs/13/13Clayton.pdf (accessed 28 March 2019).

Commissioners for Inquiring into the State of Large Towns and Populous Districts (1844). *First report of the Commissioners for inquiring into the state of large towns and populous districts*. https://archive.org/details/ b21365179_0001 (accessed 28 March 2019).

Connolly, P. (2011). 'Flush with the Past: An Insight into Late-Nineteeth-Century Hungate and its Role in Providing a Better Understanding of Urban Development'. *International Journal of Historical Archaeology*, 15.4, pp. 607–16.

Crook, P. (2011). 'Rethinking Assemblage Analysis: New Approaches to the Archaeology of Working-Class Neighbourhoods'. *International Journal of Historical Archaeology*, 15.4, pp. 582–93.

Crouch, P. (2000). 'Blind Backs and Nineteenth-Century Working-Class Housing'. *Vernacular Architecture Journal*, 31, pp. 52–8.

Currie, J. (1798). *Medical Reports on the Effect of Water, Frost and Warm, as a Remedy In Fever and Other Diseases*. Liverpool: Cadell and Davies.

Currie, J. (1805). *Medical Reports on the Effects of Water, Cold and Warm as a Remedy in Fever and Febrile Diseases. Volume II*. Edinburgh: Cadell and Davies.

Darra Mair, L. W. (1910). 'Report on Back to Back Houses'. *Parliamentary Papers* XXXVII.

Dennis, R. (1984). *English Industrial Cities of the Nineteenth Century: A Social Geography*. Cambridge: Cambridge University Press.

Dickens, C. (1836). *Sketches By Boz*. London: Chapman & Hall.

Duff, H. (1884). *Legal Obligations in Relation to the Dwellings of the Poor*. London: William Clowes and Sons.

Duncan, W. H. (1842). 'Report on the Sanitary State of the Labouring Classes in the Town of Liverpool'. In Poor Law Commissioners, *Local Reports on the Sanitary Condition of the Labouring Population of England*. London: HMSO, pp. 282–93.

Duncan, W. H. (1843). *On the Physical Causes of the High Rate of Mortality in Liverpool*. LVRO 614.12 DUN.

Enfield, W. (1773). *An essay towards the history of Liverpool*. RC RCIN 1140078.

Engels, F. (1845). *Condition of the Working Class in England*. https://www. marxists.org/archive/marx/works/ download/pdf/condition-working-class-england.pdf (accessed 28 March 2019).

Farrer, W., and Brownbill, J. (1966). *The Victoria History of the Counties of England: Lancashire*, vol. IV. London: University of London.

Farrie, H. (1886). 'Toiling Liverpool'. *Liverpool Daily Post*, 8–19 March.

Finch, J. (1833). 'State of the Poor in Liverpool'. *Liverpool Mercury*, 4 January.

Finch, J. (1842). *Statistics of Vauxhall Ward, Liverpool*. Liverpool: Walmsley.

Forster, C. A. (1972). *Court Housing in Kingston Upon Hull*. Occasional Papers in Geography 15. University of Hull.

General Board of Health (1850). *Report on the Epidemic Cholera of 1848 and 1849*. London: HMSO.

Girdlestone, Revd C. (1845). *Letters on the Unhealthy Condition of the Lower Class Dwellings Especially in Large Towns*. London: Longman, Brown, Green and Longmans.

Glen, W. C. (1952). *Glen's Public Health Act 1936*. London: Eyre and Spottiswoode.

Guillery, P. (2004). *The Small Houses in Eighteenth Century London*. New Haven, CT: Yale University Press.

Halliday, S. (2001). 'Death and Miasma in Victorian London: An Obstinate Belief'. *British Medical Journal*, 323, pp. 1469–71.

Halliday, S. (2003). 'Duncan of Liverpool: Britain's First Medical Officer'. *Journal of Medical Biography*, 11.3, pp. 142–9.

Harrison, J. (2017). 'The Origin, Development and Decline of Back-to-Back Houses in Leeds, 1787–1937'. *Industrial Archaeology Review*, 39, pp. 101–16.

Hayton, S. (1998). 'The Archetypal Irish Cellar Dweller'. *Manchester Region History Review*, 12, pp. 66–77.

Herman, B. (2005). *Town House: Architecture and Material Life in the Early American City, 1780–1830*. Chapel Hill, NC: University of North Carolina Press.

Hocking, S. K. (1880). *Her Benny*. Liverpool: Privately published.

Hole, J. (1866). *The Homes of the Working Classes, with suggestions for their improvement*. London: Longmans.

Honeybone, P. (2007). 'New-Dialect Formation in Nineteenth Century Liverpool: A Brief History of Scouse'. In A. Grant, C. Grey, and K. Watson (eds), *The Mersey Sound: Liverpool's Language, People and Places*. Liverpool: Open House Press, pp. 106–40.

Hope, E. W. (1883–88). *Assistant Medical Officer of Health Report*. LVRO 352 HEA 2/1-2/3.

Hope, E. W. (1900). *Report on the Health of the City of Liverpool During 1899*. C. Tinling and Co. Liverpool. https://archive.org/details/b29737333/

Hope, E. W. (1931). *Health at the Gateway*. Cambridge: Cambridge University Press.

House of Commons (1803). *Journals of the House of Commons*, vol. 25. London: Henry Hughs.

Hume, A. (1858). *Conditions of Liverpool, Religious and Social*. Liverpool: Whittaker.

Jones, E. (n.d.). *Direct Veto at World by the Owners of the Land*. ULSC Brunner/3/4/8.

Kay, J. P. (1832). *The Moral and Physical Condition of the Working Classes Employed in the Cotton Manufacture in Manchester*. London: James Ridgway.

Kearns, G., Laxton, P., and Campbell, J. (1993). 'Duncan and the Cholera Test: Public Health in Mid Nineteenth-Century Liverpool'. *Transactions of the Historic Society of Lancashire and Cheshire*, 143, pp. 87–115.

Koven, S. (2004). *Slumming: Sexual and Social Politics in Victorian London*. Princeton, NJ: Princeton University Press.

Lawton, R., and Lee, W. R. (2002). *Population and Society in Western European Port Cities*. Liverpool: Liverpool University Press.

Lawton, R., and Pooley, C. (1976). *The Social Geography of Merseyside in the Nineteenth Century*. Final Report to the SSRC.

Laxton, P. (1981). 'Liverpool in 1801: A Manuscript Return for the First National Census of Population'. *Transactions of the Historic Society of Lancashire and Cheshire*, 130, pp. 73–113.

Ley, A. J. (2000). *A History of Building Control in England and Wales 1840–1990*. Coventry: RICS Books.

Liverpool Corporation (1918). *Housing Report of Housing Committee*. LVRO 643 HOU.

Liverpool Health Committee (1936). *Bricks from demolished insanitary* houses: report on their use in building new houses. Liverpool Health Committee, vol. 2. LVRO 352 COU.

Liverpool Health of Town Committee (1846). *Minutes of the Health of Town Committee, 2 June.* LVRO 352 MIN/HEA 1.

Macilwee, M. (2011). *Liverpool Underworld: Crime in the City 1750–1900.* Liverpool: Liverpool University Press.

Martin Gaskell, S. (1983). *Building Control: National Legislation and the Introduction of Local Bye-laws in Victorian England.* British Association for Local History. Macclesfield.

Mata, J. D. (1909). *Habitações Populares.* Coimbra: Imprensa da Universidade da Coimbra.

Mayhew, H. (1851). *London Labour and the London Poor.* London: George Woodfall and Son.

Miller, A. (1988). *Poverty Deserved? Relieving the Poor in Victorian Liverpool.* Birkenhead: Liver Press.

Milne, G. (2006). 'Maritime Liverpool'. In J. Belchem (ed.), *Liverpool 800: Culture, Character and History.* Liverpool: Liverpool University Press, pp. 257–309.

Milne, G. (2016). *People, Place and Power on the Nineteenth-Century Waterfront: Sailortown.* Basingstoke: Palgrave Macmillan.

Moorhead, R. (2002). 'William Budd and Typhoid Fever'. *Journal of the Royal Society of Medicine,* 95.11, pp. 561–4.

Morrish, T. F. (1883). *Remarks addressed to the Mayor and Council of the City of Liverpool on the remedy for typhus; having special reference to the late report of the Medical Officer of Health.* LMI B2773.

Morrison, A. (1896). *A Child of the Jago.* London: Methuen.

Moss, W. (1784). *A Familiar Medical Survey of Liverpool.* Liverpool: H. Hodgson.

Nevell, M. (2011). 'Living in the Industrial City: Housing Quality, Land Ownership and the Archaeological Evidence from Industrial Manchester, 1740–1850'. *International Journal for Historical Archaeology,* 15.4, pp. 594–606.

Nevell, M. (2014). 'Legislation and Reality: The Archaeological Evidence for Sanitation and Housing Quality in Urban Workers' Housing in the Ancoats Area of Manchester between 1800 and 1950'. *Industrial Archaeology Review,* 36.1, pp. 48–74.

Nevell, M. (2016). *The Birth of Industrial Glasgow: The Archaeology of the M74.* Society of Antiquaries of Scotland. Edinburgh.

Newlands, J. (1848). *Report to the Health Committee of the Borough of Liverpool on the Sewerage and Other Works under the Sanitary Act.* LVRO 352.6 NEW.

Newlands, J. (1858). 'Liverpool Past and Present in Relation to Sanitary Operations'. Paper read before the Public Health Section of the National Association for the Promotion of Social Science. LVRO 628.4 NEW.

Newlands, J. (1863). *Report of the Health Committee of the Borough of Liverpool, on the Sewerage, Paving, Cleansing, and Other Works.* Health Committee, Liverpool. LMI B13825.

Newman, C., and Newman, R. (2008). 'Housing the Workforce in nineteenth Century East Lancashire: Past Processes, Enduring Perceptions and Contemporary Meanings'. *Post-Medieval Archaeology,* 42.1, pp. 181–200.

O'Mara, P. (1994). *The Autobiography of a Liverpool Slummy.* Liverpool: Bluecoat Press.

Parkes, E. A., and Sanderson, J. B. (1871). *Report on the Sanitary Condition of Liverpool.* Borough of Liverpool Health Committee. LVRO 614 PAR.

Pereira, G. M. (1994). 'Housing, Household, and the Family: The Ilhas of Porto at the End of the Nineteenth Century'. *Journal of Family History,* 19.3, pp. 213–36.

Pfeifer, G. (2008). *Row Houses: A Housing Typology.* Basel: Birkhauser.

Picton, J. A. (1886). *City of Liverpool: Municipal archives and records, from*

AD 1700 to the passing of the municipal reform act, 1835. Liverpool: Walmsley.

Pollard, S. (1959). *A History of Labour in Sheffield.* Liverpool: Liverpool University Press.

Pooley, C. G. (1977). 'The Residential Segregation of Migrant Communities in Mid-Victorian Liverpool'. *Transactions of the Institute of British Geographers*, New Series, 2.3, pp. 364–82.

Pooley, C. G. (1984). 'Residential Differentiation in Victorian Cities: A Reassessment'. *Transactions of the Institute of British Geographers*, New Series, 9.2, pp. 131–44.

Pooley, C. G. (1985). 'The Poorest of the Poor: Slum Clearance and Rehousing in Liverpool 1890–1918'. *Journal of Historical Geography*, 11, pp. 70–88.

Pooley, C. G. (2000). 'Patterns on the Ground: Urban Form, Residential Structure and the Social Construction of Space'. In M. Daunton (ed.), *The Cambridge Urban History of Britain: 1840–1950.* Cambridge: Cambridge University Press, pp. 429–65.

Pooley, C. G. (2006). 'Living in Liverpool: The Modern City'. In J. Belchem (ed.), *Liverpool 800: Culture, Character and History.* Liverpool: Liverpool University Press, pp. 171–255.

Poor Law Commissioners (1842). *Local Reports on the Sanitary Condition of the Labouring Population of England.* London: P.S. King.

Postance, H. (1884). *The Difficulties of Pastoral and Educational Work in Poor Parishes.* Liverpool: Industrial School Steam Printing Works. LVRO 283.1 TRI.

Rathbone, E. (1909). *How The Casual Labourer Lives; A Report of The Liverpool Joint Research Committee on the Domestic Condition and Expenditure of Families of Certain Liverpool Labourers.* http://www.sussex.ac.uk/britishlivingstandards/othersurveys/liverpool (accessed 28 March 2019).

Read, J. G., and Jebson, D. (1979). *A Voice in the City: 150 Years of the Liverpool City Mission.* Liverpool: Liverpool City Mission.

Rosen, G. (1993). *A History of Public Health.* Baltimore, MD: Johns Hopkins University Press.

Rowntree, B. S. (1901). *Poverty: A Study of Town Life.* Macmilland and Co. London.

Royal Commission on the Housing of the Working Classes (1885). *Second report of Her Majesty's Commissioners for inquiring into the housing of the working classes: England.* London: Eyre and Spottiswoode.

Royal Sanitary Commission (1871). *Second Report of the Royal Sanitary Commission.* London: Eyre and Spottiswoode.

Semple, A. B. (1956). *Report on the Health of the City of Liverpool for the year 1956.* LVRO M614 WAL/21/6.

Sharples, J. (2017). 'The Liverpool Origins of Jerry Building'. *The Construction Historian*, 2, pp. 2–6.

Sheard, S. (1993). 'Water and Health: The Formation and Exploitation of the Relationship in Liverpool, 1847–1900'. *Transactions of the Historic Society of Lancashire and Cheshire*, 143, pp. 141–63.

Shimmin, H. (1862). *Liverpool Sketches: chiefly reprinted from the 'Porcupine'.* Liverpool: Gilling.

Shimmin, H. (1864). *Liverpool Life: The Courts and Alleys of Liverpool.* Liverpool: Lee and Nightingale.

Shimmin, H. (1883). *Squalid Liverpool.* Liverpool: Liverpool Daily Post.

Simey, M. (1951). *Charitable Effort in Liverpool in the Nineteenth Century.* Liverpool: Liverpool University Press.

Simey, M. (1992). *Charity Rediscovered: A Study of Philanthropic Effort in Nineteenth-Century Liverpool.* Liverpool: Liverpool University Press.

Simms, G. R. (1889). *How the Poor Live; and Horrible London.* London: Chatto & Windus.

Smithers, H. (1825). *Liverpool, its Commerce, Statistics and Institutions.* Liverpool: T. Kaye.

Speakman, J., Stewart, E., Ahmad, C., and Chapman, M. (2015). 'A Community Excavation at Calderstones Park, Allerton, Merseyside'. Liverpool:

National Museums Liverpool. http://www.liverpoolmuseums.org.uk/mol/archaeology/community/calderstones-community-excavation-final-report.pdf (accessed 28 March 2019).

Stewart, E., Speakman, J. and Adams, M., (forthcoming). *Oakes Street, Liverpool: An Excavation of Court Housing.*

Stowell Brown, H. (1858). *Twelve Lectures to the Men of Liverpool.* Liverpool: Gabriel Thompson.

Strange, J. (2005). *Death, Grief and Poverty in Britain, 1870–1914.* Cambridge: Cambridge University Press.

Sutcliffe, A. (1974). *Multi-storey Living: The British Working-class Experience.* London: Croom Helm.

Symonds, J. (2005). 'Dirty Old Town? Industrial Archaeology and the Urban Historic Environment'. *Industrial Archaeology Review*, 27.1, pp. 57–66.

Tarn, J. N. (1969). 'Housing in Liverpool and Glasgow: The Growth of Civic Responsibility'. *Town Planning Review*, 39.4, pp. 319–34.

Taylor, I. C. (1970). 'The Court and Cellar Dwelling: The Eighteenth Century Origin of the Liverpool Slum'. *Transactions of the Historic Society of Lancashire and Cheshire*, 122, pp. 67–90.

Taylor, I. C. (1976). 'Black Spot on the Mersey: A Study of Environment and Society in Eighteenth and Nineteenth Century Liverpool'. PhD thesis, University of Liverpool.

Thom, J. H. (1845). *Sermon preached on behalf of the Liverpool Dispensaries.* Chapman Brothers. LVRO 252 THO.

Timmins, G. (2013). 'Housing Industrial Workers During the nineteenth Century: Back-to-Back Housing in Textile Lancashire'. *Industrial Archaeology Review*, 35.2, pp. 111–27.

Treble, J. H. (1971). 'Liverpool Working Class Housing 1805–1851'. In S. D. Chapman (ed.), *The History of Working Class Housing: A Symposium.* Newton Abbott: David and Charles, pp. 165–220.

Trench, W. S. (1863). *Report of the Medical Officer of Health on defects in the present midden system and on improvements required.* https://archive.org/details/b21971043/page/n1

Trench, W. S. (1865). *Report of the Medical Officer of Health for 1864.* https://archive.org/details/b2241227x (accessed 28 March 2019).

Trench, W. S. (1868). *Report of the Health of Liverpool during the year of 1867.* LVRO H352.4 HEA.

Trench, W. S., and Beard, C. (1871). *Working Men's Dwellings in Liverpool.* https://archive.org/details/b22298319 (accessed 28 March 2019).

Troughton, T. (1810). *The History of Liverpool.* Liverpool: William Robinson.

Turner, J. (1836). *Reports of the Agent appointed to visit, at their own dwellings, the Scottish Working and Poorer Classes Resident in Liverpool, with a view to a more efficient religious, moral and benevolent superintendence.* Liverpool: John Turner.

Upton, C. (2005). *Living Back to Back.* Chichester: Phillimore.

Vacher, F. (1882). *Report on the sanitary condition of the borough of Birkenhead, for the year 1881.* Birkenhead: Willmer Bros.

Walker, J., and Beaudry, M. (2011). 'Poverty in Depth: A New Dialogue'. *International Journal of Historical Archaeology*, 15.4, pp. 629–36.

Wallace, J. (1797). *A General Descriptive History of the Town of Liverpool.* LVRO 942.721 WAL.

Walton, J. K., and Wilcox, A. (1991). *Low Life and Moral Improvement in Mid-Victorian England: Liverpool through the Journalism of Hugh Shimmin.* Leicester: Leicester University Press.

Walton, J. K., and Wilcox, A. (2004). 'Shimmin, Hugh (1819–1879)'. *Oxford Dictionary of National Biography.* https://doi.org/10.1093/ref:odnb/50352 (accessed 28 March 2019).

Wohl, A. S. (1977). *The Eternal Slum.* London: Edward Arnold.

Index